I0079749

Alien Contact and Diplomacy: Get it Right or We Suffer

Simon Drake

Alien Contact and Diplomacy: Get it Right or We Suffer

1ˢᵗ Edition

Text and Cover Composition © 2012 Simon Drake

Illustrations within the text are used as points of reference. If infringement of copyright is suspect, please contact Simon Drake.

Written, Illustrated and Published by Simon Drake

ISBN: 978-0-9559719-5-2

aliencontact@simondrake.com

www.simondrake.com

For the unborn:
Our descendants who will leave earth,
never to return.

Here's what you can do to change the world,
right now, to a better ride. Take all that money that we
spend on weapons and defence each year, and instead spend it
feeding, clothing and educating the poor of the world, which
it would many times over, not one human being excluded,
and we could explore space, together, both inner and outer,
forever, in peace.

Bill Hicks, R.I.P.

Alien Contact and Diplomacy: Get it Right or We Suffer

Foreword

This is a work of comical contemplation, a bit like the medieval court jester joking before the stern faced King, juggling fact and fiction, craftily chortling and scoffing at the most fantastical and the plainly horrible: Good news (plentiful harvests), bad news (the plague's death rate of the peasants), or plainly how things are (the taxes are too punishing, and there's barbarians amassing at the borders). Reality, including cold reality, is best digested with warm laughter.

I have made little attempt to note historical sources, some sources are best blurred, considering the sometimes chaotic subject matter: Where and who are these Aliens, and what the hell are we meant to talk to ET about? Footnotes from the past make little difference to a fantastic event in the future that we are totally unprepared for, or possibly, unwittingly, being primed for.

Alien Contact and the logical consequence of Diplomacy will happen, or as some conspiracy theorists tout it has happened, yet only when it's out there in the public domain will it bite our soft little planet so hard and so deep we'll need to be psychologically prepared. The trauma of alien contact needs to be remedied with something unique to all humans that crosses borders and unites the messiest of foes: A sense of humour.

Alien Contact and eventual Diplomacy will be like a new dawn, but will it be like after a bad one-night stand, or meeting the love of your life?

Introduction

The church says the earth is flat, but I know that it is round,
for I have seen the shadow on the moon, and I have more
faith in a shadow than in the church.

Ferdinand Magellan

Never Forget Our History

Earth history is no stranger to the meeting of two cultures where, like the aftermath of a bad one night stand or a doomed marriage, and as the English would say (only because the British Empire seemed so good at subjugating others), one party finds the experience, 'thoroughly less than satisfactory'. History is littered with cruel jokes on unwitting civilisations, so why should our destiny among other races of the universe be any different to the numerous and in some cases wiped out, races, that walk(ed) the earth?

Alien Contact and Diplomacy is not intended to stretch the imagination with UFO conspiracies (or lack of them), nor to project utopian ideas of how good it will be when we're with them (shacked up drinking exotic cocktails with cool alien bounty-hunters etc). We plainly need to understand that when the moment arrives, we need to be prepared. And to be honest, it is an awkward subject. We don't want to be muted by our Governments' nature of denial, nor do we need to be brainwashed by our science fiction writers. We just need to be diplomatic with what will be facing us, because the end game will have amazing and unintended consequences.

At the moment, however, we aren't really prepared. There is a sense that we are, but in some ways it's like we're just waiting for our first date.

First Date, First Base

To be more precise, we're waiting for that first kiss: From sun gods to medieval dragons to UFOs and little green men, we earthlings are waiting for the messiah, the saviour, or the big Kahuna, to wander in out of the wastelands to spread goodness over our little enclave. Amen. End of story. Pass the wine and let's party. We have contact, now for the orgy.

It is hardwired into our psyche that one day something grand and astonishing will arrive. On an everyday level we have the concept of heaven where everything; life, love and wine, is an abundance and waiting for you, legs open. All you have to do is be good, or try to be good, or just repent when it fits into your busy sinning schedule. Then there is the nagging sense that one day, something big, scary, flooding or fiery, plainly apocalyptic, will roll over us and the choice will be standing on your feet fighting, or on your knees begging. Just recently the world slipped into a financial meltdown, yet in reality it just wasn't apocalyptic enough. There has to be more to our existence, and there will be.

When we make meaningful contact with an alien race, one of two things (or both, in quick succession!) can happen:

They'll show us how to unlock energy and maybe even live forever through a sharing of their technology. We can hug each other, share cooking recipes, intermarry all the taboos, tear down all the barbed wire borders around the world, and explore space without the slightest guilt that our planet is under threat. Or...

They'll exterminate us because we look funny, smell weird, and say something inappropriate to their boss. All this is irrevocable. We'll end up an unfinished footnote on a forgotten list of lost civilisations of the universe.

Why We Believe

In former times, ancient and imaginative lands such as England, China, Scandinavia, France, India, Egypt, and Arabia, have each reported a variety of dragon types. The dragons, unsurprisingly, are usually up to no good. On a slight tangent, a Saxon carving from the 8th or 10th century shows bipedal dinosaurs attacking a group of quadruped dragon looking things. In-fighting among the dragons? Not all hugs and fiery kisses? Or were the Saxons possibly documenting two breeds of aliens going fisticuffs on our turf?

Thanks to our ancestors, including those enduring the Middle Ages, their illustrating in many different lands the different characteristics of dragons, presents us with enough evidence to believe that dragons existed, yet only if you're five years old and younger. What were our ancestors thinking? Fast forward a thousand years. The dragons have retired, are lying dormant, or extinct, but we have UFO sightings, and we certainly have an avalanche of media purporting that UFOs exist, both here and in 'outer space'. In a thousand years will scholars snicker, "What were 21st century people thinking! UFOs!"

However, while UFO sightings seem to rise as a result of convincing science fiction media (think of the impact of 1950s sci-fi and the 1990s 'X Files' series), there is some evidence that UFOs are identifiable: Aliens are actually popping down for earth. Then comes the inevitable conclusion that someone made them, sent them here, and therefore has some vague plan. Why does there have to be a plan, any more than the single mindedness of many of our own early explorers. So, what is the plan? Who are these things? What can we do? What will we really do and say? Is there some alien middle class that is taxed to pay for these explorations to earth? What's their agenda?

Well, their plan, if interpreted with a level head, can't be that hard to decode, and what we do follows on from that, so who or what these things are on about, one day we'll find out. The most important thing is that mentally, us hick earthlings have to be prepared for our big date with intergalactic destiny. We have to be standing tall and firm, bright and cheery, ready to shake hands with a slimy green thing from across the universe or dodge a fireball hurled from a dragon looking thing.

Can We Really Be Prepared?

In short, how can we be prepared, when we have no idea on intergalactic diplomacy? Thanks to our own history, we have an abundance of episodes which can shed some much needed star light on the errors of decisions that have shaped our history. And this isn't just about us – it's equally about them. Some may argue it's not really equally, because face it earthlings, their intelligence will give them an edge, but they are playing on our turf. In time, when we rocket out of our solar system and befriend the multitude of species out there, our concept of exopolitical diplomacy will have moved on, but for now, we have to have some basic parameters to attend to.

What If It Never Happens?

Many things never happen, or they never happen ever again, or the same way as before. Dragons haven't been seen in a long time but it doesn't stop us from seeing them on the movie screens or in our minds' eyes thanks to vivid story telling. Some scientists, un-imaginative drones, or people who genuinely have better things to think about, prefer to assume earth is alone, hurtling through the cold depths of space with little purpose other than to look pretty from the moon. In many ways it's easier to be alone, to concentrate on running our own state of affairs, and splendid isolation is not worth spoiling. So be it.

Yet for many of us is the lingering feeling that we are not alone, and even if we pass away without having ourselves proved even a tenth right, we still know that mathematically or spiritually it doesn't make sense that we are (or were) so alone.

Please Make One Assumption: They're Out There.

To believe that we are alone is admittedly a bit of a great lonely leap what a curse to be so alone! However, there is little proof to believe otherwise. Science fiction and questionable UFO sightings keep the fire alive, yet they can't truly be believed. At some point you have to shrug off the sceptics and the bogus sightings and decide that we're not alone. From then, a whole new train of thoughts come hurtling from out there down to us: A sense of galactic responsibility.

Note: This book may explain why we may have been 'left alone' and therefore, tragically but not irreversibly, just 'left behind'.

How does anyone really know if we are alone in the universe? Well, they don't. But the debate rages a bit like the flat world concept: It just must be flat because, 'well, everything around me is very flat'. And naturally at the edge of all flat world concepts (or maybe conspiracies) is the great 'falling off the flat world fear'. Yes, you sail your ship to the end of the world and simply fall off, you come crashing down and land among all the other ships (and maybe dragons) that made the same simple mistake: Assuming the world was round. If we are alone in the universe then the same is true: You steer your super Star Cruiser in one direction and soon or later you'll fall out of the universe, probably onto a flat world, without meeting anyone interesting on the way.

Back to earth, back to reality: The boffins (scientists) are discovering exoplanets: planets outside our solar system. Space is not a void (the great nothing around the flat world map) and is populated with stars, planets and a host of things we know a little about but will one day study in great detail. The feeling that we are alone is probably more a fear than an acute observation, but to the credit of those who can work up the chutzpah and wail, "We are alone – get used to it" is the fact that as far as we know, no alien species has opened a consulate or trading post on our planet. Sadly, for the moment, apart from conjecture that we are not alone, we have to rely on some solid form of evidence.

There are UFO sightings from credible people; and while it's understandable that it's not in their best interest on an intellectual and career level to admit seeing something odd in the skies, sometimes they do step forward and point over yonder and say, "Even though I am sane and trained to fly expensive machinery or operate advanced aerial surveillance technology, over that way, there are UFOs," which can be as detrimental to one's employment possibilities as saying, "At 279°, 10,500 feet, are a fleet of dragons, flying figure eight patterns at approximately 500 miles an hour, apparently flirting with some prettier dragons who maintain a steady course south at 290°, 10,000 feet."

Interesting UFO sightings, maybe because they spark the imagination and in aggregate form the sum of all fears; monsters and ghosts and dragons, do present enough evidence that aliens are out there and indeed visiting us. However, this is no need to bang the drum that they're here: If they are, we don't see any 'public' sign of them, so they're as good as not here anyway. Thanks for nothing.

In order to make speed and to enjoy this dialogue, accept the assumption that they exist. You don't have to believe they walk amongst us, control our lives, run our economy or ride around in spinning upturned dinner plates, you just have to accept that:

They're out there, and then,

They're riding around in upturned dinner plates, may have an influence on our economy, and can one day influence our lives.

And Why Would They Bother With Earth

For the discerning exploratory alien, when you're so brainy, so knowing, and obviously advanced enough to have mastered the pillars of intergalactic frivolity and stability; endless energy, securing your home planet from destruction, and the technological ability to surf the stars, how are you then to fill your time? In all probability the universe will end, so for any advanced culture sprawled and yawning across the vastly empty universe, no matter how intelligent or bored with us they are, they still need some excitement and purpose: Alien races will come here out of a sense of curiosity because what else are they to do? Life is about exploration and with Earth's abundance of species, even a little venture now and then would yield something curious and therefore marginally valuable to an alien.

The next and more dramatic thoughts are, if they come here out of curiosity, what is the nature of their curiosity? What eggs them on? Where does it lead to?

The answer to this lies on many levels, and these answers, as well as the sometimes bizarre questions that get us there, must be appreciated because one day they'll help us understand those who have travelled a long, long way, to meet us.

Early Extra Terrestrial Interactions

"The US Air Force assures me that UFOs pose no threat to National Security..."

President John F Kennedy

Too Many Non-Events?

Before embarking on diplomatic relations with aliens they might have to make the first step. Flying around in spinning hub cubs, giant silver cigars and other assorted 1950s sci-fi paraphernalia, and making little sojourns to biologically interrogate livestock, shine little three-pronged lasers up a poor soul's quivering rump, collecting a few plant specimens and then buzzing a commercial jet airliner for a laugh, is not actually 'communicating' anything special to us. If we believe the victims of such occasions, it is indeed good for a laugh and in total can be passed off as just another questionable contact in a series of non-events. A real event would be an alien Star Cruiser rocking up into earth orbit and showering us with trinkets: each trinket would have some power over us, emboldening us with a wondrous technology or ability.

Suspected, documented and celebrated alien activity to date is interrogative, not a meeting of cultures, and can be passed off, or is it a sign of something on the horizon?

You'll Never Believe What I Found

The duckbilled platypus is a unique Australian, yet when early explorers brought it back to Europe as a specimen, zoologists thought it was a hoax and that some enterprising explorer had sewn a duck's bill onto a baby beaver's body and attached flipper hands from some other animal. Only a live platypus could be believed. The whole idea of returning with specimens is to give your patrons a taste of what is out there and an incentive to probe further, so the fabrication of evidence was one way to prove one's mastery over sea and land and have your wild dreams of adventure, fame and fortune, fully financed. Yet when you are capable of reaching out across the cosmos, truth will be stranger than fiction every time.

Specimens spark the imagination, and even though ET probably has a brain at least a thousand times more efficient than yours and mine together, he/she or it must still have a sense of curiosity. The museums of the world are packet with jars of things, many brought back by explorers who bravely wandered into unknown worlds, hoping to make a great discovery and probably ending up as a footnote in history and with a weird looking bird named after them. An alien race, and alien individuals too, will have the same sense of adventure. Again we have to wonder, what is life all about, what can their life be all about? Inside all of us is a collector or some sorts. Is something out there collecting from us?

Wow, Listen to This

To any alien drone posited in the solar system for eavesdropping and weather reporting, the burst of radar activity during World War Two may have caused it to prop one eye open and tick a box: Wow, those pesky humans have discovered radar. Yawn. Add this to the list of human discoveries: Fire, the missionary position, the wheel, beer, stone tools, red wine, bronze spears, white wine, iron armour, the croissant, steam power, air power and then flower power.

You have to assume for a second that they are listening to us, and it's not that hard. Let's say you're an alien, you reached an adequate form of intelligence a billion years ago, and you like to know what goes on. You litter interesting planetary systems with self-replicating and self-repairing devices to listen in. Somewhere on your dashboard a little light flickers and a drone mumbles, "Those carbon-based bipeds are sending junk into space."

Naturally enough you'd listen in and record everything. Thanks to satellite communication, you'd have access to tonnes of earth media and phone conversations that it'd take an alien brain the size of the Titanic to interpret. And interpret and correlate is what an eavesdropping drone must do, because it must report back. But what kind of specimen has it found? How much daytime TV soap opera from across all earth's cultures (Latino, American, British, and Australia – to name a deadly few) and constant news coverage can it stand before it self-destructs? And if it listens in to international phone calls, does it get excited about the juicy calls; long distance extra-martial affairs and high stakes international diplomacy, gone wrong? In the last decade the internet has exploded, so does an alien have to sift through that mess too? Imagine ET slumped before one of box shaped computer screens, scanning hundreds of millions of boring Facebook profiles, tedious graphomania blogs, amateur porn websites, listening to millions of talentless music tracks on MySpace, and snickering at Google's infantile search logarithm. What will it discern from this? How will it categorise what's important to us, by bandwidth, by searches, by actual pages? It will detect a wide spectrum of boring tirades, a herd species that revels in its stupidity thanks to countless YouTube videos, yet what will it make of spam? A valuable human preoccupation or just robotic babble? When it comes to new inventions, would Viagra rate higher than Solar Power? What message would it send to its master other than a nauseating moan?

Or it may just tick another box. Humanity has crawled like an air-head, shaggy-haired, drunken art student into the information age. As a specimen we are probably fun to poke yet an artefact; in aggregate a piece of art. What we tell them about us (including our shame) can only be positive: Hit and miss as we do, we like to communicate, and we do.

Assumption: We Mean Something to Them

From the flesh to the email spam, from the genes of starfish to all six episodes of Star Wars, you have to assume that aliens have at least some of it bottled in glass jars or whizzing around in their memory banks.

What they make of it all, who knows, but one thing is certain, apart from maybe abducting the unfortunate (or just imaginative) and maybe eavesdropping (or perhaps wincing and turning the other way) what they have learnt from us is not enough to stage a public introduction. To date, there are no Alien Star Cruisers beaming us better television programs, programming a more efficient system for the organisation of the mess of the internet, or trying to preach their Gods to us. To sooth our deflated sense of intergalactic worth, the reality is that we simply haven't ticked enough boxes, and the last one is probably this: Humans have discovered real space travel.

Although we may not be on any alien cultures' diplomatic priority list, if you believe that at least once in the last 100,000 thousand years an alien spacecraft has flown by, and perhaps made a follow-up visit, then you can be sure that we mean something to them. What that is, how it works out for us, will bring about change and throw a giant mirror into our faces: What do we mean to them, what do they mean to us, and what are we really on about?

And what will we be able to actually say?

Realities as Diplomatic Parameters

*Any sufficiently advanced technology is
indistinguishable from magic.*

Arthur C. Clarke

Who Are We Anyway?

The first chapter of the Bible is called Genesis. It is a story of how the earth began and how we humans, and of course all the wildlife in the world, were created. Although it is as much a work of fantasy as an Aboriginal Dreamtime story (where giant snakes slither through the land creating the paths of rivers), we shun the illogical aspects and keep on with the story, because without the Bible, we wouldn't have Christianity. It's not too sensible pulling religion into any debate about Alien Contact and Diplomacy, but it is worth noting that it was Christian oriented countries that led the way in the space race. That these countries are also 'drinkers' is something else not worth muddling over when you sip your vodka, patriotically scanning the night sky for a Soyuz capsule.

Religion offers an easy explanation as to why we're here. The renaissance unshackled us from religious subservience and led to a scientific explosion that now allows us to probe the beginning of the universe, our DNA, and secure our future. In a parallel universe perhaps the Roman Empire never faded away, it prospered and tinkered and without the slumbering Middle Ages in the way, perhaps the Roman Empire would about now be dispatching a legion to Alpha Centauri or going head-to-head with some alien species you'd read about in an obscure science fiction novel.

Instead, it's just us looking up with powerful tax-payer funded telescopes, scratching our heads, obviously alone, many questions completely un-escapable, and we believe we are not alone because it's a good topic to keep us awake at night and it seems an unbelievably (and illogical) curse to be the only 'intelligence' in the entire universe. Then there is the disparity between the unproven and the very, very improvable theories about who and what is 'out there' and what they're doing down here, even what they're doing to us. This self-generated noise may eat into the deafening silences that we hear from the universe, but we are genuinely curious to know the reality and our place in the cosmos. To date that's as good as it gets, and yes we can better ourselves by reaching and exploring the cosmos, but we're not there yet. We prefer to spend our money on other things, like pet food, because our four legged friends do a good job at keeping us company. We could elect to spend more of our money on technology that would enable us to listen in a lot better to the noise of the universe (SETI is leading the way in this front) and then maybe we'd pick up an alien phone call. Even when we do detect something intelligible, and manage to unravel it, what would the contents be but a snippet of conversation between two aliens who are having nothing but a mundane chit-chat:

"How are you?"

"Good."

"Been awhile, huh?"

"Suppose."

"Seen any funny black holes?"

"Nah."

"Me too."

"So.... What are you doing for the next 3.164 thousand years?"

"Not sure, might visit earth, for like, a laugh, know what I mean."

"Oh yeah, how about we meet there?"

"Uh, well, hmmm."

"Go on, we'll tear the place up."

"Sounds neat then, see you there in let's say 2.691 thousand earth years?"

"Hang on, I'll just check with the misses."

"What? You are such a fossil, really."

We could even shovel more of our money into technology that could shoot our dreamy minds out of this solar system and into another. At the time of writing, NASA's Voyager 1 probe, which is about 17.7 billion kilometres from Earth, is entering a "transition zone" at the edge of the solar system. Voyager is going where no man-made object has ever sailed – the space between the stars – and out into the galaxy. That's as far, and as good, as we've got, and at the moment, Voyager doesn't boast much of a plan.

And what, if beyond our trite efforts, 'they', them aliens, are here, over there, or ruminating on how to talk to us? The reality of their existence and efforts crush our efforts and if ignored, becomes our loss, and even our peril. The quirky possibilities of how and in what form they are out there shape the parameters of any potential diplomacy. It's up to us to pre-empt the unknown.

We Are From Them:
And Therefore Their Property

Creationists, swallow your pride for a second. We could be the offspring of aliens. Remember the Sky Gods the ancient scripts banged on about, well they're our great grandparents. Try re-wiring your faith around that.

We may be part Neanderthal, part something else. We could just be a refined version of our shaggy haired, sloping browed, dull ancestors. Or, by alien design, they're not our ancestors at all! Thank God, we can relax! We may be an experiment or an insurance policy, we may be the pets and we'll never know the truth until we pry it out of the universe.

So what happens if this is the truth and what do we say to it?

From a legal point of view, if we were designed by aliens and planted here on earth, are they our parents? Do they have, in the eyes of an intergalactic court, rights over our souls? If so, we'd have to fight to establish a sense of uniqueness that separates us from our owners, and a right to exist unmolested from our 'breeders'.

On the plus sign, if we are the product of a successful breeding experiment, then the master hands that guided us would surely be looking after us? If we are in times of need, would they help?

If geopolitical fisticuffs escalates into the widespread use of nuclear arsenals (battlefield use of tactical nuclear weapons on a limited scale won't annihilate us), with the forecasted result that life on earth would be snuffed out under a radioactive cloud, would Alien Mummy and Daddy come down and negotiate between the warring parties?

Another catch to being the property of some unknown species is that if we prove too troublesome, we can always be sold or passed on. We can use nuclear weapons on the battlefields of tomorrow and never wipe ourselves out, we can pollute our ecosystems with less than apocalyptic results, and we can over populate our planet to the point or catastrophe, yet earth will bounce back in the long run. We may tarnish planet earth as damaged goods, and inevitably play a hand in forcing the hand of our owners into doing something completely unforeseen, like making an appearance to enforce some discipline, or yes, selling us to their neighbours at a discount.

This scenario drives the need for alien diplomacy to new levels because we need to know our own rights when they own the rights to us.

They Walk Amongst Us

Aliens have long been suspected to walk amongst us. Those hyper-sensitive to the issue will claim that persons in high places were placed there by certain races of aliens. Others will tell you that they are indeed the aliens, and for a fee you can join their little group that has VIP tickets to the mother ship, which incidentally is coming next Tuesday after morning tea.

On a more prosaic note, if aliens are amongst us, we are left to wonder: What are they doing here? And if you are an alien amongst us, reading this, many people feel very sorry for you: What did you do to deserve to get this job? Draw the wrong straw? Say something that at the time seemed funny, but ended up infuriating or embarrassing your superior? Is being sent to earth a demotion or punishment? Or are you the anthropological type, gathering information? What a tough job, wearing a human skin (unless of course you designed us), sometimes eating crap food just to appear to fit in with suburbanites. Or perhaps you're a high ranking alien embedded in the United Nations or something just as lethargic, the European Union. We feel your pain for all those bureaucratic meetings your super intelligent brain would have to sit through, biting your tongue every time some career public servant makes some mind numbing point that triggers two hours of non-stop nauseating banter. Human suicide may be simple compared to your suicide process – do you have 'a way out' from walking amongst us? We may never know the full tragedy of being an alien operative on earth. Many unexplained suicides may be alien operatives who've just had enough and couldn't wait for the mother ship to pick them up and send them on a well deserved holiday.

However, if there is a job to be done, then the aliens amongst us must get it done.

They're objectives may be surveillance, information gathering, or being the silent hand that guides us to a better future.

Our relationship with them may be so open we may not even know it. After all, they would be well aware of our distressed situations and be able to implant the required means to pursue solutions. For example, new technology that has aided us to explore our earth may have been passed down by a superior race; much to the annoyance of our own scientists.

If aliens do walk amongst us, then they also have near complete control over us. They do not require diplomacy; they only need to influence us in their direction. The chilling aspects of this situation is the basis for many science fiction horror stories and for good reason: It just sounds too horrible to be true. Alien(s) would control our thoughts; run all the lobbying firms and high-end PR companies, plus the banks... Let's not get started.

They Visit

A safe place at the table to meditate on 'aliens and us' is that they come and visit, in the name of science, having a holiday, or even a cute little picnic.

It's a safe punt because it involves little commitment to engage with them, and there is minimal action required from outside. Humans like things just the way they are. We don't want the concept of super-intelligent life out there arriving and shattering our belief systems. It's just too much of a headache, yet when we're bored of our earthly existence, we can get excited, much the same way as our peasant ancestors did with dragons, about UFOs.

Many UFO sightings are faked. With an early version of Photoshop, an hour of creative thinking and application, then 5 minutes uploading your creation, you can implant on the internet a blurred, obscure UFO buzzing some out-doors place on a nice sunny day. Why is that most UFOs are seen in standard weather, and never in the rain, or in a storm? Why can't UFOs fly in the rain? What's wrong with their technology? Lack of windscreen wipers?

Then there are, as we all know, the piles of evidence which point to UFOs as very unexplainable objects with true intelligent design and very unknown intent, which draws out the question: How do we deal with them? You can't, or to date, they won't. So, sit in that safe place and enjoy the speculation and entertainment. At least they visit, and this will lead to a climax, some sunny day.

They're Out There, *Somewhere*.

Statistically, someone is out there. The exact parameters (and there are many) that enabled us to crawl out of the primordial sludge were the same somewhere else out in the universe, most likely (10 billion years ago) before our planet started forming (5 billion years ago).

If an alien species conquers space travel and bothers to say hello to us is one scenario, yet the other is a touch lonely – we may have to do the exploration and forcing of ourselves on alien cultures. Either way, we're over here, they're out there. Sounds like two frigid teenagers at a really lame party.

Accepting that aliens are indeed out there is the safest place to be because it requires no effort. The universe is accelerating outward and the party is just warming up. As long as we survive we can encounter them, and vice versa. Viewed in this light, it almost seems too easy that an alien species should arrive, let us in on their world, and gleefully answer some of our greatest questions. Perhaps an alien species only makes itself present when we've actively proved that we're out there too, and we'll meet you in the middle.

They're in our Solar System

The nearest star is Alpha Centauri, 4.242 light years away. We won't get there in my life. We won't get there for a very, very long time, and it's the same with most stars: Between them is the void, space. Travelling through space is not just skipping from here to the moon, it requires the conquering of time and distance. If an alien species can do that, who knows when they passed through and what they left behind. And if they're not here on earth, then for the sake of stereotyping, let's squint at Mars; Mars forever bearing the brunt of our fears. Mars, where until better telescopes extended our view and imagination, seemed like the best possible place from which organic extraterrestrial malevolence could spring from. On the assumption that aliens, and this could be a civilisation or a listening post, are in our Solar System, we can concur that they know we're here, yet they're reluctant to open up an Alien Burger

Franchise and sell us bottled water containing the finest asteroid water in the solar system. If they were close and numerous, they'd want to trade something. If all that's in our Solar System is an automated drone ticking boxes as we evolved physically and mentally, and as our civilisation advances without snuffing itself out, then we just have to wait until we do something proactive that triggers the drone into action.

For those with a vivid imagination and a powerful telescope at their disposal, there is talk among the believers that on Mars in the Hebes Chasma there is life. If you spot life, well done! If you can spot a row of heavily armed flying saucers taking off, call your local emergency services number.

They're 2 Cool + We R Way Boring

You get the picture. You feel the vibe. You're just not hip. Hard core alien civilisations evolved well over 10 billion years ago, some right after the big bang. And earth? Well, 5 billion years ago earth came together and managed (or did it?) to coax some chemicals into life. There's not much you can say to an alien intelligence that is 5 billion years ahead of you. Anything you say will be un-cool.

We earthlings will either have to find other aliens just like us, or that are a tiny bit older and don't mind the attention of a younger cousin or friend. If we're over here, they're over there, and just as lonely, shunned by the older, ancient, cooler alien cultures.

Let's Hang Out in the Middle

Finding a slightly more advanced than us, or just a less advanced than the most advanced old school aliens, band of benevolent aliens that genuinely wants contact is probably the only realistic end game when hunting for contact.

While the desire to make contact from at least two races is required to get anywhere, the technological means to do so and where we meet in the middle is where the magic will happen: Contact is a meeting in the middle. Contact, like receiving a signal (SETI is working on this, and you can too by joining them) relies on the alien sender having the technology that operates on a wavelength that we know how to receive. Forget for a moment that if we do pick up a packet of data we'll be scratching our heads like Muppets trying to make sense of it (unless it comes with a translation or Rosetta Stone), contact from far away, via detection, means that we're on the same wavelength, until of course they grow out of it, as we have done – analogue gives way to digital and then what?

Inter-galactic Body Language

If they exist (they do), and how close to us they really are (who knows), are nice starting points. So let's say the gap is closed and we have contact. The best way to formalise a meeting of cultures is with a meeting, and here comes the crunch: What are they?

All the old highly identifiable signs of body language during moments of diplomacy will probably have to go right out the window, or airlock, when dealing with aliens. They may read into our body language, because they've studied us by sending a scout to craftily watch and takes notes of the actions of desperate humans at the card tables in Las Vegas. Therefore, we can assume that in any face-to-face meeting, that the greatest tricks and ruses of our orators, mediators, and television savvy politicians, will be close to or near useless. Our inter-human diplomacy techniques are all about us; reading us, lying to us, bonding with us. This is not to say an extraterrestrial race that has endured the journey here doesn't want to communicate, it just means there are obstacles even before we can shake hands, break the bread, and send our favourites concubines into the others' beds.

Inter-galactic Bodies, or Lack of Them

Spare a moment and examine your thumbs. We humans have opposable thumbs that can touch any digit on any finger. Some animals also have a kind of opposable thumb, or even toes, and opposable thumbs are a feature of the primate family. Unsurprisingly, the humble opposable thumb played the crucial role in allowing us to use crude tools and then later the invention of more cooler, craftier tools. No opposable thumbs equals no axles and therefore absolutely no wheels. No wheels equals, way, way, way down the line, no wheels for space shuttles to land on. We, at this stage, rightly assume that to get anywhere in evolution, like off the jungle floor, a species needs opposable thumbs, or maybe just more arms and hands, or maybe just a neat row of impressively long, slender, eloquent yet sturdy fingers that enables a species the ability to 'tool' its way out of a very predictable and possibly dead-end existence. So, the next time you're abducted by an alien, be sure to prod his or her or its hand and see if the thumb is opposable. If it's not, some of us are very wrong and we have much to think about after dinner. If the thumb is opposable, science fiction speculation wasn't that wrong: Yet why do we assume aliens will look like us? Why do we assume they'll have two legs, big brainy heads, and arms, with fingers! And opposable thumbs!

Take a dip into the water, and while no known species under the waves has developed the wheel, there are quite a few species that have bodies completely different to ours. It's therefore perfectly logical that out there in the cosmos there are planets with widely different atmospheres and seas, birthing wildly different species to that of ours on earth. At least one of these unknown species will have had the drive to break out of it cosy little world, create its own kind of space craft, and push the limits, perhaps billions of years before our distant relatives wormed out of the seas.

Regardless of the wild planet and the wild body of this Unknown Species, all it has to do is tool materials to get going: How it does it is as yet no concern to us. However, it may very well be a jellyfish that does it.

Now comes the crunch: How will you react to a superior being that may look to us like a misplaced bowl of translucent spaghetti? Will you be able to believe in love and peace with an extraterrestrial force if they arrive looking like conjoined octopus, each scooting around in its own anti-gravity powered glass bowl that contains a liquid that looks and smells like a drug addict's urine? Will our leaders of our most advances cultures and masters of our media, including those that have kissed snotty nosed babies for pre-election posing, be able to shake hands with a scaled, three-eyed, giant bug-looking thing, from outer space that reeks of sulphur and breathes only methane?

Now for the Talking

Nightmarish body contact aside, successful exopolitics will rely on some good old chin-wagging between Earthly Elites or whoever is around at the time, and our Brand New Friends from Very Far Away. How to break the ice when there are not only cultural difficulties, but a complete difference in language, and even a perception of time?

The difference in communication methods are limitless. They may speak through channels we can't detect, or in wavelengths we're not use to, like tones of light, by touch (via their mucus covered, fish smelling, 17 fingered, hand thing), or by a squelchy sound only audible to dogs (which would enable man's best friends the upper hand and then we'd be their little pets). They may prefer inter-galactic ceremonies to take an hour or two so they can slither back in their Super Star Cruisers and zoom over to Mars in time for teatime at their Forward Operating Base, or it may take decades, conversing in milliseconds every few months, just to build a shimmer of trust.

So Let Them do the Talking

Without proper preparation, we'll have to let them learn Earth ways, pick a language or two, and they can stutter their way to some middle ground. Their language may simply be beyond our scope, we may rely on an ET invented translator. In any case, as we're not reaching across the galaxy learning their language, we'll expect they'll be apt at it, or if it's their first time, ready for it. As English is the language of international business, it may well be quotes from Shakespeare that are chewed over by alien tongue.

> *They have been at a great feast of languages,*
> *and stol'n the scraps.*
> *'Love's Labor's Lost', Act 5, scene 1, 32–39,*

William Shakespeare

The Tyranny of Distance

It's important to ponder if they're out there and what they look like, parallel to the question of, are we even remotely in the right place? Think of space as from here to eternity, and then some more. Are we going to meet anything vaguely interesting in the middle, and vice-versa? The vast distances of space are sometimes conveniently ignored, and you only have to look at the space between the visible stars to get some idea of how gigantic space really is. But aside from this slight misery, it is worthy to highlight a few physical restrictions which shape the parameters of an alien diplomatic envoy suavely touching down in Times Square and handing out the blueprints for top of the line, energy efficient, interstellar propulsion systems.

To those who still need to be reminded, space is, well, space: Massive, empty, cold, and to us, inaccessible. Most astronauts get as far as low earth orbit (about 320 kilometres) and the last time anyone kicked the moon was about 40 years ago. For us earthlings, the cost to counteract gravity hinders our space activities. Sure we have better things to spend our money on, and if you're on the receiving end why complain, but if you are, please bear in mind the exorbitant cost of space travel. There are tonnes of reams of paper written and to be read on this subject, and only commercial space initiatives can change our ways. Now cast your mind to an interstellar civilisation that has conquered this distance and lives to explore. Some enterprising spark replies to a round table discussion on who to visit next with: "Planet earth!"

And then the bean counter accountants assess the situation: Who should be taxed to fund this venture? Pick on the least wary.

Meanwhile, a crew is being asked (or programmed to respond to) a question like, "How do you feel travelling for seven hundred years in a deep freeze to see a blue planet?"

What if it were a ten millennium ride? To a free thinking space traveller, would you sign up for a mission that would be a great sacrifice, or perhaps space travelling species factor in the tyranny of distance. While we bang our heads against low earth orbit and think a mission to Mars is long (years, not months), aliens are zipping around the universe, and most probably their bodies are built for the task, enduring missions that span an epoch of history that covers the time between our ice ages.

A Painful Assumption: You can't travel faster than the speed of light.

Why is this so painful to assume? Because it makes die-hard science fiction and fantasy fans cry themselves to a bitter sleep: Sorry guys and girls, but travelling faster than the speed of light breaks the laws of physics. If it was possible to zip through space our little blue planet would be bombarded by intergalactic tourists and intrepid alien theme-park executives searching for the next galactic attraction. You wouldn't be reading this, you'd probably be enslaved to one of these forces, polishing their boots, cleaning their toilets, or at its best taking them on whale watching cruises and wearing a dumb T-shirt. So, thank the limitation.

Now that we have swallowed that bitter pill, look around the universe. Stars are anywhere between 4 and possibly infinite and thus incalculable light years away. Imagine coasting along fast as a sun beam. That's the speed of light. Does the ability to travel twice, or even half, the speed of light, change much? Until an alien gets here and lectures us on one or the other or both, assume not.

If you were a civilisation on a distant star and you gave the green light for a venture to earth, your craft's top speed and travel duration might be longer than your crew's life spans, sanity limits, and the craft's technical expectations. Out there in deep dark space, anything can happen.

Just look at the voyages of the early explorers, many of whom we don't even know about because they set off across the ocean and disappeared; fell off the edge of the known earth. Their place in history is missing because so are they: They never returned to regal us with tall stories and grotesque specimens. And for the alien trippers, it might not be much different, but let's give them the benefit of the doubt and say they made it here. It took them 10 years or 10,000 years, and time isn't what it is to us, but still they made it.

After travelling so far, and resigned to the fact they may never return the same, or if they do return their world will not be the same, are these aliens expected to behave? They could be robots of some sort, programmed for optimal best behaviour, and even then the creators and investors of the venture would want something in return. Are specimens enough? Apart from information (like the saturation and mind numbing data flood of the internet) and technology (which are still primitive to a higher and dangerous intelligence) the nature of specimens from earth haven't changed much in the last 10,000 years. When it comes to flesh, what more can you find, except for lesser species, than before?

Whoever, whatever, and whenever they get here, we must understand they've come a lot further then we ever have and in the immediate future, will. We'll be mindful of their conquering of space, but not forgetful: The depth of the journey for many early explorers, like the Christian Crusades and Spanish conquistadors, shaped the outcome of their exploits.

The journey and the destination become one.

OK, Assume Space Travel is Relatively Simple

The author can acutely hear the groans as the readers, scattered throughout the world and hopefully one day the Solar System, and then perhaps in an inter-galactic beer garden, contemplating the preceding section and sigh, then moan, "But travelling faster than the speed of light just has to be possible! It just has to be!"

Well, OK, you win. Travelling faster than the speed of light, jumping in and out of worm holes, riding the chocolate tunnel of a black hole – it can happen. And a whole lot more. Freaky alien beings can flip between dimensions like a hooker doing multiple tricks in a night. Supreme beings drift, in their lifetime, from the centre to the outer rim of the universe and then back again, absorbing and wiping wisdom about all along the way. The universe is not only as fantastical as all the steaming creative produce of science fiction writers who have actually made money out of their work, but it is also incredibly amazing as the steaming creative product of science fiction writers who have made absolutely zero money from their work. The universe is wild, limitless, and we're still sitting in the corner, alone, wondering, picking our noses.

Have we been left behind, or are we yet to catch up? Did someone drop by and then leave, and we can only decode the trivial evidence left among the ruins of ancient earthly civilisations that are buried deep, or at the moment jack-hammered apart to make way for high-rise apartments? Who knows, who cares? All that matters is that in a reality where aliens do travel faster than the speed of light, and therefore faster than a whole lot of other things which will pester our scientists for a long time, we're still here, alone.

Indeed, aliens might be here on earth, whizzing about unseen, but as the public don't have any real contact with them, what's the use? Again, until an inter-dimensional craft that can travel 10,000 the speed of light (and a whole lot of other things) arrives and takes some of our modest leaders for a ride (and hopefully deposits them far, far away), we have no idea of this kind of capacity. We may be so far behind this capacity that any species that has mastered it, simply drives on by as you do, through the countryside, completely unaware of a certain ant colony on your right, only 300 metres away, called earth.

An Alien's Point of View

While we were at work there came nine or 10 of the natives to a small hill a little way from us, and stood there menacing and threatening of us, and making a great noise. At last one of them came towards us, and the rest followed at a distance.

William Dampier (Explorer)

How Would Aliens Decide to Visit?

For a technologically advanced species to be aware of intelligence other than their own, recognise an opportunity, then venture on a trip across the galaxy, prepared to endure the tyranny of distance, and then survey an alien world for a substantial duration, and hope to return, requires a lot of manpower, or extraterrestrial power, including labour, funds, and a whole chain of decision makers and layers of dreamers, fans, lobbyists, scientists and fund raisers.

For all those decisions (why to visit, when, what to send there, what to wear, what to expect, risk analysis, worst case scenarios) requires the worst fiend known to great ventures – a bureaucracy. The Alien Bureaucracy To Investigate Planet Earth probably began as a few fanatics with crazy notions who had accidentally swung their experimental antennae our way and detected strange transmissions from a strange quadrant of their observable galaxy; they could easily have tuned in to a cheaply produced soft porn film beamed on a pay-per-view service via satellites and thought "Savage creatures but strangely interesting". Then this motley fascinated crew obtained funding from a humble sponsor to investigate further, evidence of intelligence on earth grew and then so did the interest and therefore finances, so it became a lean and astute task force that scaled up with excitement and fervour and spread and splurged into a cumbersome and lumbering bureaucracy

Yes there is a purpose, and yes their efforts to explore other worlds may not be limited to Planet Earth. They may launch one or a hundred ventures per their year to the space dusty corners of the accelerating out universe, and intelligent as they are, there must be order underpinning every excursion.

They want to know what's out there and for us, their strength is also their weakness. Yet any advanced alien species will have to abide by some code of conduct.

Distillation comes with civilisation, which leads to science and technology, which can never exist without bureaucracy, which monitors the laws (and intergalactic taxes (and intergalactic tax avoidance) but that's another book, in a galaxy far, far away).

Alien Visitation Rules of Engagement and the Joys in Breaking Them

To visit earth, that is to reconnoitre and verify what they have heard or suspect, requires a steering committee abiding by protocols. What laws visiting aliens have when probing earth and buzzing earthlings, and how each visiting alien interprets these laws, can be seen by believing the most credible evidence of alien interaction. A good place to start is the case of alien abductions. If the stories are true, then we can ascertain that for some aliens it's within their remit to pluck an earthling out of their sleepy farmhouse, cart them off to a mobile laboratory, and shine an assortment of lasers in their orifices. If these acts are within the rules for aliens making an excursion to earth, then so are others, like buzzing commercial airliners and travelling parallel to cars traversing across sparsely populated deserts. To date, an Alien Star Cruiser has not, from afar or near it doesn't matter, directed a laser to our most contemptible (e.g. nuclear missile silos) or favourite objects (e.g. the Eifel Tower) and obliterated them, then enslaved us. So far, so good.

Yet with all things mechanical, some day they break down. The much hyped Roswell incident, in which apparently a UFO crashed, may be proof that even Alien spacecraft are not 100% reliable. And with all things intelligent, sometimes they think they know it all and can do it all. If you were an alien, so far away from home, and possessed some degree of free will, would you not find some enjoyment in doing something a tiny bit naughty and off the record? Isolation breeds temptation. Perhaps much of the unexplained can be perfectly explained, and the culpable are probably flying back to their distant star with a sneaky smile on their merry little face.

Obligations for visiting aliens must include the golden rule: Don't destroy anything. This rule, and it must be true if aliens have visited earth because there is little or no evidence that aliens have destroyed anything, shines a soothing light on the grace that intelligence produces. There are countless Greek and Roman statues missing arms, heads, genitals and anything else an invading horde of barbarians could hack at with a sword – vandalism is a sign of either bad behaviour (lack of grace) or low intelligence. Grand acts of vandalism are sometimes blamed on grand people, like the fabled shooting off of the Sphinx's nose by Napoleon's troops, yet to date few have stepped forward to say "The Aliens were behind Pearl Harbour to start World War Two and for less effort and equal satisfaction brought down the Twin Towers to kick-start World War Three".

However, to every rule there are exceptions: Preservation. According to Robert Hastings, author of 'UFOs and Nukes', aliens have disarmed nuclear weapons with the simple intention of reminding the military that these weapons are a bit too dangerous for our feeble intentions. While the world is awash with conspiracy theories, and military personnel are reluctant to testify against the hand that feeds them, if aliens had been disarming nuclear weapons during the Cold War, it would be because part of their rules of engagement must include that of pre-emptive intervention: Stop the earthlings from turning their cities into glass bowls (craters).

Specimens

Most exploratory voyages have a scientist on board, and if they are someone who really likes to push the boundaries, there are rewards. Exploration and specimen taking breed outcomes other than just fancy glass-jar collections of the exotic and unimaginable. On the 27th of December in 1831, Charles Darwin began a voyage on the HMS Beagle that lasted almost five years. While the Beagle surveyed and charted coasts, Darwin investigated geology and made natural history collections. His experience and notes, coupled with reading from other sources on the subject, over time, challenged and then shaped his views on our creation. Yet it wasn't until 1859 that he published his theory on evolution in his book On the Origin of Species. By the 1870s the general public accepted evolution as a fact. He was not the only specimen gather in that period, yet his outcome helped us to understand ourselves.

A specimen gatherer also knows their limits – they are not to interfere with local power politics. A specimen hunter, though, would be more adventurous, because with intelligence must come egotism and a sense of adventure, so at some point something or someone interesting should become a specimen (if only for a night or an hour) of a visiting pro-active alien biologist.

Alien Communication Lag

Conspiracy theories are great, and like tales of dragons, punctuate the monotony of our day with the surreal and unexpected. And truth may be stranger than fiction, but reality trumps all. Imagine an Alien Mother Ship is dispatched to our solar system to 'observe but not obliterate' our finest technology, our evolution, our political factions, the mentality of our superpowers, the speed at which we're wiping out other species, and a host of other things that are recorded mercilessly on our ominous Intergalactic Report Card.

From the Alien Mother Ship drones and manned craft are sent in for a closer look. In 1945 they observe World War Two brought to an early close by two nuclear strikes; until those tragedies the allies confronted a greater tragedy in terms of possible body-count: Invading Japan, house by house. Forty years later, in 1985, the guardian aliens observe the nuclear arms race and the shifts of power behind it, and decide to intervene on a low level, that of disarming nuclear weapons (as speculated earlier). Between 1945 and 1985 is forty years, and if a message takes 20 light years to go from the Alien Mother Ship to its base, and 20 light years to come back, we can assume they're out there, and not that far away, processing us. On the other hand, an Alien Mother Ship may be here with the protocols set in stone, it may not have to confer with a higher authority on intervention and diplomacy.

In any decision making process, where events lie out of existing protocols and planning, an intelligent species should 'talk with the boss' before making an adverse decision. The big 'if' for earth is, and something that must be clarified as soon as possible, is that with any aliens wishing to be diplomatic, how do they communicate with the organisation that sent them here? How far away is their headquarters, their paymaster, and their wife?

If an Alien Ambassador arrives, does it take a thousand light years to send a message back and forth? May their own civilisation have moved on while they have been busy coming here and observing the savages?

However, we should trust that any alien species that goes to the effort of coming this far must have thought long and hard about what to do when here. They may have seen species come and go (think of the asteroid strike that did in those poor innocent dinosaurs) many times before, and are mildly amused by the struggles of humanity (or just humans), and it may be thousands of years before we present a situation where an observing Alien Mother Ship has to radio home, "The fur-less bipeds on Planet Earth are getting pretty interesting and funny, can we say hello to them?" and then wait however long for a return message. By which time we've either snuffed ourselves out or pioneered interstellar travel.

Contact Outside of Earth

In all probability and plausibility, why would a space travelling species want anything to with a species that can't yet travel through space.

First the benchmark: How do you define space travel. Visiting your local moon? Colonising a planet within your solar system? Is that when the spinning hubcaps appear before our leaders and a ramp extends from the silver belly and a little green beauty queen emerges with a wreath of exotic flowers and sings a song of congratulation?

Earth history reached a revolutionary peak when nations came in contact via the seas, and the technological prowess to cross space and time then led to culture clashes that are integral to our history: Missionaries were trying to convert savages, explorers and merchants were trying to barter their way towards a specific objective: Get rich or die trying. As usual, he who was there first, apparently has the first claim. Therefore, when we get to Mars, should we be surprised if a UFO zooms down, and walking down the ramp is a little green lawyer from a far off planet explaining that we're trespassing on some civilisation's boondocks property? Do we then pay some fee for arriving, a fine for staying too long, and a toll to let out adventurous selves leave?

On a more realistic level is the temptation that out there in our Solar System is something left behind, or dormant, or mundanely observing us. Impetuous to get out there and find out is just to know the basics – are we being watched and by what – is it active or passive?

Active Observation from Within our Solar System

As scary as it is plausible, and yet it would make sense considering the depth of space and how tiresome it would be to visit here on a whim: What if aliens where in our Solar System, actively observing and visiting us? What do we say to them when we finally locate their little hole-in-the-asteroid or secret moon base camp? First we have to find out exactly how far they are from home, how long it takes them to send a message, because they might call in the cavalry, they might just call it quits and head home once discovered. If there is an outpost, and all they can do according to their rules, is observe and mildly discourage us from wiping our planet clean, how would the populations of the world react to benign guardian angels? Will they get a seat at the United Nations? Shouldn't they contribute to our humble space efforts, like how Christian Missionaries shed the light on the tribes in the darkest of jungles?

Passive Observation from Within our Solar System

Given the scenario that any active and inter-stellar civilisation is a few billion years ahead of us, and not very interested in us until we experiment on a level that gets their attention (like create our own patented black holes for fun), they can sit somewhere in our Solar System, watching, waiting, perhaps anticipating, and definitely yawning. And what's more frustrating is that it's their job to be non-detectable – what fun would it be otherwise. It's up to us to find them, prod their drone, tow it back to earth and sink in a few diamond tip drills to see what it is made of. However, that won't be possible. A civilisation that is even 5,000 years ahead of us would know how to create, dispatch and monitor drones that are harder to break than anything we could engineer. If they're out there, they have the advantage.

Defunct Relict from Long Gone Alien Civilisation Rusting in our Solar System

No arctic wasteland or patch of baking desert is complete without the remnants of someone who got there and not much further. Seeing rusting cars on back roads in remote areas is a nice reminder that if aliens arrived here before we learnt to walk upright, and stayed here, they could easily be here, but died of boredom just as we were learning to crunch on the lice evolving in each other's cracks. The concept that aliens may have visited earth or the Solar System and left something behind, died on duty (that is, dying of boredom or killing each other out of boredom) should act as a temptation to get out there and discover. What defunct and rusting alien memorabilia could be there? An outpost on Mars? A sulking, lonely drone waiting to be recharged? We won't know until we go.

Contact Outside Our Solar System

The next space race will be to spread humanity within the limits of the Solar System.

The commercial draw behind such expansion is just beginning, and this new age and revolution may last a few hundred years. If, in the process aliens still haven't made contact, humanity will begin to ask itself some tough questions, the most obvious being: Are we trying hard enough?

Then the next space race will be a lot more ambitious. Depending on the technology around, space explorers will push out, first to set up bases and colonies on the closest of stars, and then within a few centuries, shoot off to a few more stars a bit further out. And on and on. And on. And on and on and on, until one day, space travelling earthlings run into space travelling aliens. When and where this will happen is not worth getting too excited about because you and I will be dead and atomised. We can suppose it will happen like many a great occurrence – by accident, or 'pure arse' as some modern Brits like to say.

In 1788, Captain Arthur Phillip had sailed the First Fleet (made up of mostly convict vermin from the streets of London) from Great Britain, to Botany Bay in Australia. The British were far, far away on the other side other world from Europe. Their intention was to establish a prison by populating it with their cargo of convicts. The British are an odd species, and using a prison on the other side of the world as a deterrent to serial criminals on the streets in

London seems absurd, but so are the juiciest parts of history. Yet eight days after anchoring eleven ships in Botany Bay, finding it unsuitable, and then sailing out, who should swan into the bay, but two French ships?

Lapérouse was leading a scientific mission (not quite an absurd reason to travel so far), financed and ordered by King Louis XVI. From historical accounts, the British and French were very cordial. On the other side of the world, who wouldn't be? Sadly Lapérouse and his ships sailed off to a demise amid a cyclone somewhere in the Solomon Islands, never to be heard of again. Apparently Lapérouse and his crew were stranded, most of the crew tried to reach civilisation and never made it, and Lapérouse died shortly before any real help stumbled upon that part of the world again. Captain Arthur Phillip had a different destiny: The British, after leaving Botany Bay, settled for a cove in Port Jackson and established their colony, in what is now known as Sydney. Australia turned out to be a mineral rich bounty, adding greatly to the British Empire. The French had their revolution and ceased their wild explorations, while the British made a great empire and to this day still import many things from Australia (iron and soap operas) and sometimes export televised royal weddings.

The lesson is that the adventurous, on their own errands and with their own intentions, will run into each other, eventually.

If an alien species never knocks on earth's door, or has left a marker somewhere in the Solar System for us to stumble over, there is consolation in the hard reality that we may have to find them out there, when we're in the process of doing something else. Somewhere, at some point of time, our hard work will pay off.

What Are We to Them?

For where your treasure is, there your heart will be also.

Matthew 6:21

The Infinite Means the Intangible

Let's begin with a real downer, something horrible and negative.

Ever wondered why after years of living near someone, you've never really spoken to them? We all have non-relationships in our lives; colleagues, neighbours, fellow members of the community, that we see sometimes, and never, ever, want to know. Don't fret over why, it's just that you and them have absolutely nothing in common. To even strike up a casual conversation is painful, and both parties cringing, if not simmering, are thinking but never connecting, 'I shouldn't be partaking in this obligatory contact'.

And so it will be with alien species, near and far, who see earth and rate it as either Too Painful to Make Contact With or it's just very, very low on the list of places to visit in the infinite universe.

Because of infinity, or if that's still too hard to imagine (it is) just the many planets out there supporting more groovier forms of life, there's an extremely high diversity of fun filled intelligent life forms with 'lives of their own', and many, even if they could spare the effort, still don't want anything to do with us, even if forced into a cage with us.

In the wild, animals co-exist without too much socially awkward interference. Predators and prey tie each other up with the old game of hunt and be hunted, but beyond that game of survival, and excusing parasites, different types of animals don't seem to be hanging out together; being social and friendly because they feel responsible for the well being of the jungle, savannah or desert.

A superior alien species owe us nothing. Perhaps we should then become parasites.

However, things can't be that bad can it? If there are supremely intelligent beings that rate us on par with ants and dust clouds, then there must be not-so-supremely intelligent beings that will, out in the infinite, take an interest in us.

More than a Specimen – A Curiosity

Now and then, thanks to syndicated 24 hour news, two minutes of very important prime time television news, sometimes just after the weather report, is devoted not to the latest local and international body counts, but to the re-discovery or major discovery of some long lost tribe deep in the darkest heart of the most exotic jungle (usually the Amazon) or an overlooked island. No microscopic report is complete without a zoom in on a tribal man hurling a spear or aiming a poison tipped arrow at the intruding intrepid camera man and brave reporter. From a distance we can see they're primitive. If they're menacing or peace loving is irrelevant but just markers, and it makes us warm in our hearts to know that even though our modern lives are confusing, erratic and tiring, there exist a few scattered tribes who have it simple, and bless them, we hope they never have to change.

In the Bay of Bengal on the island of North Sentine is a 'lost tribe' of Negritos called the Sentinelese, surrounded by growing economies and trade routes. They're not that lost; from the beginning they were feared as cannibals by Arab and Persian traders, have shunned all attempts by the Indian government to make contact, survived the tsunami of 2004 (maybe they caused it with a new kind of rain dance) and even as late as 2006 impressed the world's news editors (and a few ardent environmentalists too) with their archery skills on two fishing men (you're not a local, are you) fishing illegally within range of their island. When a helicopter came to retrieve the bodies of the fishermen, it was met with a hail of arrows.

Let's assume that's how aliens see us: Primitive, a little bit funny, touching, and living the simple life. When they come and visit us, we scramble our slow, cumbersome, fossil-fuel-fed fighter jets steered by characteristically High Octane Ego Driven Hot Shot Fighter Pilots to do our first stage of diplomacy.

We think our world is advanced and a bit crazy and hectic, but in truth, not much has changed, just the transportation, the communications, and the weapons. We are still a bunch of tribes, most in peace, some in war, and some half asleep. Perhaps we are confused by the concept of the noble savage, that if we came from savages, we've left that skin behind, and can triumphantly look back on our ancestors as 'noble' to atone our vicious path. There is no noble savage, 'The Horror!' of the savage is genuinely cruel: High infant mortality rate, susceptibility to diseases, banging your family and friends on the head with blunt instruments, torturing your enemies, the tribe at the mercy of nature, isolation hinders innovation; severe isolation means you're stuck in the Stone Age behaving like a pack of dogs even in the 21st Century. Earth's isolation means critical innovation must come from within, and quirks in our own innovation will set us apart from the competition.

But back to the savages, it was the meeting of the Stone Age savages with the 'superior' and 'altruistic' that inevitably led the 'noble' savage to be worse off. This is not the rule, yet many aboriginal tribes (Australian Aboriginal, Maori, American Indian, Inuit) were at some time going to encounter explorers, crusading missionaries and finally well meaning settlers of some sort, eventually carving up their land into suburbia. Where the 'invaders' came from is irrelevant, history could have served up different outcomes; if the British Empire hadn't so vigorously mastered the seas (by allocating a nice chunk of their 17th and 18th Century GDPs to maritime supremacy), the French or Dutch would have, and I'd be writing in French or Dutch, rather than Australian English, mate. Without going into further gritty details about the clashes of the have-nots and the have-a-lot-mores, history shows that the meeting of the primitive and the advanced is no fairy tale.

Aliens view earthlings as curiosities because to land here and show us the intricate workings of a ray gun and share inter-galactic mutations of influenza will have predictably disastrous results, backed up by reports from similar excursions on similar peoples gagging for intergalactic frivolity. Are abductions part of a controlled process to see what happens when two (or more) species meet in the one room, and whenever a UFO plays catch me if you can with a fighter jet, are they just taste testing the tips of our poison arrows and exploring their delightful findings with an inter-galactic news network that's gagging for something to fill their own mundane slots? Even aliens need some light entertainment after the Space Weather Report.

If you can assume that aliens have interacted to a limited degree with humans, by prodding our bodies and teasing our most advanced weaponry, then you can digress that there is a next step, and they may hold great expectations for us.

The Up and Coming Teenager

Optimism is intelligence. The trials and tribulations of modern history are akin to that of the teenager. You can judge a teenager as an extraterrestrial can judge earth. ET's checklist for earthlings gets more advanced as we advance:

Earthlings have so far:

1. Invented very, very dangerous weapons,
2. yet have not destroyed themselves with these very, very dangerous weapons.
3. Pro-actively decided to protect their planet from themselves,
4. and avoided the unnecessary loss of too many species.
5. Respected the origins and management of their own species,
6. without interference from the non-verifiable religious beliefs of their own species.
7. Ventured into space, explored the planets in their own solar system,
8. and wish to explore the stars.
9. Visited other star systems, encountered other forms of life (other than their own),
10. and managed not to in all their excitement to bring danger and destruction to these life forms.

Earth's maturity is not so far off, but not that close either. On many fronts there is 'promise':

✓ We have treaties on the large superpower stockpiles of nuclear weapons, and can sleep relatively easy knowing that the casualties of a terrorist nuclear attack or a rogue statue going to nuclear war on its neighbours would be 'small change', as Napoleon would say.

✓ Environmentalism has taken an active footing and is evolving from a fringe cause into something it always naturally was: An internal organic drive to protect one's sanctuary.

✓ The United Nations, European Union and other layers of organisation do bind our tribes, and the timely demise of radical religious groups will herald a new period of international harmony.

✓ The Moon landings, future Mars landings, the upcoming age of exploration and commercialisation of our own solar system will take time but the fundamentals are there.

When Earthlings do venture out there, we'll probably be quite pacifist – indeed any civilisation that hasn't killed itself off in its formative years will be passive, perhaps explaining why earth hasn't been invaded yet.

Perhaps the sign that we have matured is when, like teenagers, we're over ourselves getting over ourselves – and then we'll be ready for the ultimate coming of age party: Space.

The Rites of Passage

All notions of goodness, tree-hugging and harmony aside, modern history is stained by the lethargic bungling of the Middle Ages. Why couldn't Rome have kept its course, and if it had, we'd be exploring the stars by now and trading slaves with aliens. Sadly, the lost millennium of the Middle Ages happened because it's a lesson: It can happen again. And there's little reason for it not to.

A few slips in geopolitics can cause rifts deep and wide enough that the plentiful use of nuclear weapons, and weapons not yet invented, could cause the decades of decay that Rome went through in, a matter of weeks or months. Be it general nuclear destruction and nuclear winter, or a meltdown of civilisation and dawning of anarchy, it is all tangible. The proof that it is possible is in the stockpiles of nuclear weapons, that actually act as deterrents. Yet the nuclear threat may never dissipate, this yoke around our necks may follow us into space, but to a visiting alien who wishes to make a lasting impression other than gathering specimens, what incentive is there to deal with a species that can wipe itself out? It's almost like teenagers subconsciously shunning loner destructive teenagers: Awkward personalities breed their own problems. Proof that we are really 'so over' the destructive capability of ourselves will be an internal Rites of Passage that leads us to external adventures.

Unique Value

What, apart from specimen taking, is of any worth on earth? Because of the isolation of earth, there is no trade between earth and some other planet. If an alien wishes to break into the earth market they really have to do their homework; raw materials are available in asteroid belts, we're only as credit worthy as our Gross National or Intergalactic Product, we trade amongst ourselves, and we have enough salty water to drown ourselves with if the earth overheats. So what would an alien culture really value on earth? Why would they come so far and make contact? The answer is simple: What they can't generate themselves.

Artefacts

Look around upmarket antique shops in the wealthier quarters of towns and you will find artefacts from far flung places you're probably not brave enough to venture to. If you fancy the carved pieces from Papua New Guinea, you're impressed by the originality of the depiction of whatever it is; crocodile, God, warrior, mother, something phallic. It may have been carved last year, or five hundred years ago. All you know is that where that thing was carved, you probably wouldn't survive more than a week. What you don't purchase is an ubiquitous object that you can pick up anywhere. You want something unique, and whether it is an artefact or a piece of art, it adds another reference point to your collection. We seem to relish anything from some exotic culture, so earth artefacts would be no different. Somewhere in the culture quarters of a city that lies at the heart of a grand alien civilisation, is the Earth Museum. It's only opens Monday to Thursday between 10AM and 3PM (except for lunch between 12 and 1:30), is funded by a dribble of generations (ex-astronauts who after visiting earth and returning several thousand years later, decided to allocate a tiny fraction of their pensions to something memorable), and staffed mainly by volunteers (who dreamily entertain themselves that they were meant to be born to live the simple life on earth). In this Earth Museum are artefacts: An ape called Lucy, a Neanderthal, a Homo Sapien, a Roman Centurion, a Samurai, a cat, a dog, a condom, a Coke bottle, a sabre and an Exocet anti-ship missile. The collection is just 'stuff' that visiting aliens have managed to pilfer without upsetting the inhabitants. Next to the Earth Museum is also the Earth Bar, where you can meet private collectors of earth and other inhabited planet artefacts.

If there is a trade out there, some of our stuff is changing hands.

Artworks verses Digital

We all collect art. Even if your only collection is a stack of low-IQ films, what you collect mirrors your own retarded ways and your seasonal attempts to address it. Now transplant your brain into an alien culture that is so over itself, so over everything it knows, but the thirst for knowledge never dies. It lives on knowing more, it thrives on new discoveries. It may even thrive, on modern art, from earth, the type of modern art that looks like vomit, no matter which way you rotate the canvas.

Apart from modern art, which is sadly almost a non-art; more like a performance, art is robust. An oil painting from 500 years ago can be viewed by anyone with eyes. A mobile phone video clip uploaded to YouTube exists only as long as there exist the software and hardware to view it.

At another extreme, we may be art, a creation, and in the end, our DNA a string of code.

While our output is interesting relative to our development, digital output and the explosion of it, is also collectible. Everything is art in the eye of an alien, much like when a tourist visits a far off place everything looks so amazing and interesting, even street signs and street lamps. However, durability, a solid art form (like a painting or a sculpture) is better than a digital creation because digital requires power, and the power that an alien culture would use will be way beyond what charges your iPad.

Everything about is Primitive

The innocent splendour of primitives is an ageless attraction. We gape at apes in the zoo, whales in the open sea, and surviving stone-age cultures that haven't fully morphed. We crave simplicities (stick that in your Tweeter account). It would be no different for a visiting alien when they look down on us. Therefore, any of our artefacts, be it a Big Mac or a hand grenade, a pair of high heels and leopard skin tights, it has value to some collector back at the Earth Bar or in his alien hometown.

For us though, we have to accept that we are viewed as primitive, there can be little digression beyond our incapability.

Technical Artefacts

Compare an ancient single-hull Viking boat, with a twin-hull Polynesian craft, and a Super Oil Tanker. Visit a museum containing pre-modern medical instruments; saws, forceps, and other contraptions we hope to never ever see, because thankfully these days we have effective anaesthetics and modern sterile medical instruments.

For those who like to collect, art is one brand, and technology is another. Viewed from afar, old technology is art, it definitely surpasses bad art, and it easily slots into the narrative of development, discovery and ingenuity.

What different aliens races would value from earth is hard to speculate, but you could suppose all the craft that have vanished from the Bermuda Triangle are bottled up in a giant collection somewhere, complete with crew and pilots.

As earth continues to develop, we will remain a target for technical artefact hunters. However, if the exponential rate at which we develop new technical marvels continues the surface of the earth will be covered with patents, the wires leading to their devices, and earth will resemble a metal clad ball. So, even as our development levels out, we will always have something to offer.

Fossils

While we can pride ourselves that if aliens come they come explicitly for us, it is worth remembering that 99.9% of all life on earth died on earth. The vast list of species is obliterated by time, but there are fragments of fossils, that tell a story.

Our story, the recent and most exciting to us, is perhaps 5,000 years old. And while our story accelerates, our species doesn't. A visiting alien would be interested in the species that preceded us, as much as the most intelligent of earthly species, us.

An alien fossil hunter would also be interested in recovering evidence of life that might predate their own (if possible) and that runs parallel or ahead of their own. The comparison would be valuable as a reminder that life anywhere is a struggle, a grind, full of many dead-end species, but we are not alone, and made it. *Champagne!*

Playing our Diplomatic Cards

Our aces are the unique things that we produce. Does this mean that if aliens arrive in a cordial and pompous fashion we shall offer gifts of our finest art, artefacts and fossils? Why give something away for free when the true value is yet to be ascertained? How much is the oldest stone age wheel going to fetch at auction on the other side of the known universe?

In any event where aliens are coming and they appear friendly, the best gifts we can give are not our most precious, but just a few levels below. Sure, give away a partial dinosaur skeleton, some three billion year old fossils, jousting swords, duelling pistols, a centurions helmet, a Warhol, a Picasso and an iPad – they've probably already got them. But there is no need to impress by giving away the best.

A Shopping Mall

Some of the best cities are traditional trade hubs; New York, Hong Kong, Singapore, Venice, Amsterdam, Frankfurt, to name a few. An enterprising alien, and an enterprising earthling, should see that above the diplomatic niceties (giving gifts of cultural importance) is the gift of inter-galactic independence – the ability to make a dollar from foreigners. What is this shopping mall, other than selling earth art, artefacts and fossils? Does it become a pawn shop for struggling aliens who make it here and can't afford to go any further? Who cares. All that matters is that for earth to get out and over its self, it needs to start trading with others. Most minerals can be found in asteroids, but pretty postcards can only be found on tourists strips. If anyone can make pretty postcards of earth, it's earthlings. If the aliens do arrive, make a t-shirt or a hat for them, use a silk-screen to print on the slogan "I Love Earth and Earth Loves Me", and then you can sleep at night knowing you're made a difference.

Bottled Emotions (as Specimens)

Great art depicts scenes and emotions. Great books and movies follow the changing of emotions and situations. The usual hits are love, contest, and hate. The act of love is depicted by romantic kissing or to the other extreme, hard core smut. When it comes to contest, it's the heat of the competition; from plays about family rivalries to television series about professional challenges (picture in your mind televised glossed-up high-powered lawyers unleashing their power-egos). Then the act of hate, from sweeping paintings of ye' old Man of War cannon laden ships going toe-to-toe, to trench warfare, gas chambers, to B-grade chainsaw massacre movies, there's no shortage.

As the audience we are tricked into feeling an emotion; we're not really in love with the fairy tales Princess nor are we running instilled with fear from her chainsaw wielding tormentor. But we do pay a lot of money to feel these things. They are integral to our well being. Emotions are also universal in intelligent life. What drove the great explorers to the ends of the world must propel the great space explorers to this side of the galaxy. And for a superior race that has seen it all; explored it all, tasted it all, shagged it all, and exploited it all, what apart from specimen collecting do they have to do? And what would be the best specimen to collect that is alive? Objects, like art, are dead. They are static. But for a superior alien race to freeze time on emotions in action, and re-run them in their own little galleries, would be a feat that is technologically possibly and possibly as boring and mundane as a modern art video installation. The act of two humans making love, or in a duel, frozen in the moment through some mind and body control, can't be that different from re-watching in slow motion a boxing match or savouring the close-up on an Alpha Bitch (e.g. Heather Locklear in *Melrose Place*) in a soap opera. We enjoy it. So must they.

We're a Consolation Prize

The great colonial land grabs by Portugal, Italy, Spain, Belgium and the imperial masters France and Britain, left Germany, by the time it was unified enough, with little to grab. As late as 1884 it annexed the Bismarck Archipelago, a group of islands off the north eastern coast of New Guinea in the western Pacific Ocean. The islands and a few other small conquests were in comparison to other empires a small consolation prize that Hitler, seemed to try to rectify with World War Two.

The area around Papua New Guinea is rough, at the end of the known world, and the people are as far removed as you could imagine. As a fledgling colonial power, explaining to them that they are being conquered because 'everyone else has been conquered, enslaved or enlightened' and that 'if I don't someone else will' must be a bit humbling, so let the Bible lead the way and face the consequences later.

Fast forward to the now or the future and we have earth, possibly far removed from the geo-political action of the universe, but still a destination and an object worth something. Like a tribe on an island in the Bismarck Archipelago, are we destined to be sucked up by some species who think they have no other option but to get in first in case someone else does?

If we are the bait for an alien's civilisations jealousy, it gets even worse. We may have even be overlooked by the very advanced alien species, so our first real contact will be with a lesser of the alien species (think: Klingons!) who are out to prove a point. Prepare to be enslaved, and thankful for it.

Outcomes: The Good, The Bad, the Ugly, and the Weird

When the missionaries came to Africa they had the Bible and we had the land. They said "Let us pray." We closed our eyes. When we opened them, we had the Bible and they had the land.

Desmond Tutu

The Good

If only it could all be so easy. If only a benevolent alien species could simultaneously land on all the lawns of all the nations' White Houses and Parliamentarian Beer gardens and Parade Grounds and Grand Palaces and explain the fruitful secrets to ever-lasting governance, a less than nauseous form of democracy, and straightforward environmental sustainability. Like peasants rejoicing at a Spring Fair, all the world's leaders would applaud their alien friends and make a jolly dance. The peoples of the earth would drop their funny religions and wacky customs and embrace reality: God is universal, we are not alone, there are things out there greater than us, and they're nice people too. They're here to make all the evils of earth dissipate into the ether. So let's explore infinity.

There would be exchanges of technology so revolutionary that earth would never see children starve or become obese, the fundamentals underpinning our economies would change to something so alien and passive that nations would no longer feel the need to sink then saw their teeth into the others' throats. Gadgets and industrial scale revolutions would solve all energy needs and earth would never again experience over or under heating due to suspected manipulation of greenhouse gases. Last, but not all, over-population would recede like the wave that it is and all the cute, colourful or fuzzy endangered species in all the precious coral reefs and rainforests could continue procreating in ignorant bliss of how close their line had come to an end. Or, humans could continue to breed like rabbits and colonise other worlds, the settlers of the future living out exotic yet wholesome sci-fi pioneering fantasies.

Earthlings would live happily ever after. This fantastical utopian concept is strangely what most welfare recipients live on: The government saves them, because apparently it and all it stands for owes them, yet this reliance causes resentment. But the aliens would solve that too, maybe transplanting the brains of the non-believers to a salt mine in some far off galaxy. The end goal is all that matters: Earth is saved from itself. Close your eyes and pretend it just might happen, and when you open your eyes you'll be slave in your own land.

The Bad

It's all bad. If you wake up in the morning and see an invasion force of UFO's waving a pirate flag, and your most admired politician trying to placate imminent apocalypse by waving a crude flag with a dove and fig leaf (peace, man) at the alien bastards, hide under your bed and hope it all goes away. Don't worry, it's probably just a dream or a vision.

The ramifications of any contact, be it the receiving of a seemingly harmless yet intriguing signal by SETI from way outer space, or an actual meaningful visitation that is digressed correctly and leads to the unanimous acceptance that extraterrestrials exist not just for the commercial purposes of Hollywood studios, will change humanity forever, and for many that's bad enough. Close your eyes and not just imagine, or believe, but recognise 'they' really exist. Now extrapolate on this. What a headache.

The good news is that many people can relax, "Thank god we're not the only Muppets in this universe! Do you think they fancy a drink too?"

Unfortunately, the step of accepting there are other worlds will lead to all sorts of calamitous activities, many of which are so mind numbingly obvious and boring its best to look at them in a sober yet cynical light:

Does God exist for Aliens? Is he a she or an it? Does he, she or it, love us more than them? Did we offer sacrifices to he, she or it, before they did? He, she, or it, is our God! Let's fight over it!

Are we at the mercy of these beings? History has shown how intermingling cultures usually leads to one on top, and the rest eating cold slop. Let's fight to be number one!

Any foreigner is Unwelcome. The repulsion at foreigners is part of our species, and though multiculturalism has shaped our opinions away from rampant hick-style racism, don't forget that someone killed off the Neanderthals. It was probably our long gone ancestors, out-witting the numb skulls, to rule the wilderness. Upright two legged species have most likely been clubbing each other over the head since day one, so fight the whimsy notion that two-legged, bug-eyed aliens will be providers of love and grace for the needy and be above beady eyed malevolence. Lynch them.

Sadly, it is the isolated savage, fearful as he is ignorant, that can view an alien interaction as only a horrible episode best avoided. Alien contact, and how we interact, shows a mirror before our faces, and the reflection alone, perhaps because we may not speedily or agreeably recognise our own maniac grin, unsettles us into all sorts of calamitous states. Beware the barbarians at the gates.

Tune in to any media supplier of greed and conflict: wars, proxy wars, petty disputes, and ceaseless body counts – if it's not broadcast analogue it's certainly receivable digitally – the barbaric 'newsworthiness' of primetime and the billions it coaxes, should be a gentle cue to any gentle space borne aliens, that earth is a troublesome blot in the pristine emptiness, but not unconquerable, depths of space. Even our modern history, like the organised slaughters of World War One (where 19th Century military tactics of marching men in a line to the enemy, in this case being the 21st Century machine gun) highlight a gaping lack of intelligence in the mightiest powers that were.

Therefore, we simply can't hide the barbarians in us, and therefore those 'superior' aliens may discriminate against us, for being us! All the more reason to ban that old treaty banning the positioning of weapons in space – we need our weapons in space to keep them aliens bastards and their alien bastardising ways at bay! How dare they expect to change us, alien bastards!

Now take a pause.

Up to this point, the alien bastards haven't done anything un-towards little helpless earth. Were an alien bastards species to do something mischievous to our little blue droplet in the dark, cold void of space, we'd be helpless. Any civilisation that masters space has the technology to annihilate us, but luckily for us, the 'bad' aspect of our solitary stance in the universe, is primarily ourselves. Once we get over our own reputation to ourselves, then we can begin to contemplate alien contact far from being plain wonderful or apocalyptic.

The Ugly

An ugly situation is where you have little control over the environment that is creepily changing around you and the outcome that is creeping from behind on you, and last not but least, the bucket of shit you'll have to eat for not having committed suicide yet. An Ugly outcome of failed alien contact and diplomacy might not even appear that ugly – we may think earth has some stature in the universe, but then find out that the particular stature is fraudulent, as are the motives of our new inter-galactic friends.

History is littered with ugly little affairs, easily glossed over, yet it seems a constant: Right now, on some part of earth, and in many parts of the universe, some benevolent species is shafting some slower, naive, nicer species. Diplomacy is the art of getting 'what you want' without letting the other guy 'smarten up to how much he's being screwed'. It's all a charade. And if a visiting alien civilisation is up to tricks, it'll most likely be ugly to us. We'll wake up one day with a giant hangover yet unable to articulate how we got into such a painful state and unsure who exactly was in our bed.

Alien maliciousness is not the only cause of an ugly earth changing episode; alien kindness can just as easily cripple our beliefs and turn us into a bunch of mad monkeys; not that hard since we share 99% of the same genes.

The Weird

What have we learnt about history? What do we know about our own experiments, whether we knew we were experimenting or not? Bankers and bureaucrats are equally guilty for their numerous experiments yet at the cost to someone else, the customer and tax payer, respectively. The bankers make a bet on how much the rest can borrow and repay and profit even if their clever house of cards falls away. Bureaucrats make wild guesses countering the way things are and create social experiments, determining how generations of tomorrow will have to live with each other upon the basis of radical new concepts that exist for the sole purpose of trying something new to disprove tried and tested notions of the past upheld by an old guard. Yawn. Intelligent and ingenious species make experiments, and regardless of the motives, we live in the outcomes. Everything around you is the outcome from something seeded long ago, or maybe just yesterday. Throw in the joys of chaos and randomness, and the variations of Alien interactions multiplies and each demands a shifting diplomatic response. Mutations occur in all plans. When humans face a cousin species, it won't be just to drink tea and marvel at the weather. We'll have been left behind and angry about it, keen to make up for lost time, get very teenage and competitive, and want to sleep with them.

There are of course fear, joy and common interests. But there is also the vast unknown between us that could magnify and exacerbate the unexpected consequence of our meetings. Negative outcomes are easy to tally: Earth 0, Aliens 1.

Positive outcomes are easy to speculate. At the top of the pile is a cosy win-win scenario that's easy to swallow and spread as a meme, e.g. 'The Aliens are coming with super cool technology to improve our shitful condition! We're saved from ourselves!' could one day be a cry to out-do the Christian belief that Jesus died for our sins, therefore everything is going to be OK.

Unexpected outcomes are intangible and extremely harder to accurately express. We can't forecast exactly what is out there, and the parameters that guide their interaction with us. This makes diplomacy extremely hard. However, for some form of guidance, we can look at our own interesting torrid, and sometimes quirky and unique, weird history.

After all, the most interesting history is that which doesn't make sense now, but at the time shaped the destinies of empires.

Possibilities

All genius is a conquering of chaos and mystery.

Otto Weininger

An Introduction to Historical Random Acts of Worst Cases

Ever been wiped out by plague, an accidental genocide, ripped apart between two or more feuding 'worlds'? These are some of the nasty side-effects of coming into contact with aliens. Fragile ecosystems are always under threat from some parasitic horde deposited from afar; there's enough evidence to show that the clash is a constant, and adaptation equals survival. On a cultural and race level, wise Native American Indians can probably raise their hands to the job of Diplomatic Relations with Beings of Unknown Intentions because they've seen it all.

While the nitty gritty of history is not always pleasantly digested, luckily it's in the past, will one day (when the stretched universe folds in on itself) be forgotten, and if you're smart, you can dodge it when it repeats itself.

Earth, by very little effort of its own, is just another civilisation on a pretty blue ball that can too easily be kicked around in a game between alien personalities and cultures. Who knows, the rights to explore and extract the heat from the molten core may already be going to auction at some inter-galactic clearing house. Again, rather than wildly speculate, we can always rummage through the history books for a glimpse of previous first contacts that may one day help us to deal with our first real inter-galactic contact.

Diplomatic Pre-Emptive Solution: Form a task force to assess the findings from the following experiment: Lock up the most creative mathematicians and science fiction writers in a mountain retreat with access to unlimited food, low grade acid (LSD), fine red and white wine, German and/or Czech beer, and soft drinks. Give them a month to draft up 103 possible episodes where aliens actually come to earth. Get them to map out all the 'eventualities' that could happen, and what we should do to be prepared.

Beware the Laws of Cosmic Nature

Before we get too carried away on some of the possibilities that may fall from the sky, it is worth remembering that while we are familiar with the (sometimes loose) laws of human nature, at our base is the guiding hand of mother nature, which is a cosmetic way to deter us from thinking about nature, as in 'laws of the jungle' kind of nature where microscopic alien hordes of parasite fall from the skies onto our scalps and squirm through our ears to eat our brains. The Laws of the Jungle are just descendants of The Laws of Cosmic Nature: Eat or be eaten. Protect or be protein. We are all preying on something.

Right down to the molecular level, things are eating up other things. Little creatures evolve to deceive or completely disappear. Parasites, in all shapes and forms, the villain kind, the loving kind, and the prosaic kind, are all intent on sucking away while exerting the least of effort. If we forget the basics of the jungle, then when playing diplomacy with aliens on a noble level, we are just lowering our level in the food chain a few notches, and perhaps that's no great problem: There's lots of room at the bottom, not so much at the top (but the view is definitely better).

We're Waiting to Be Converted

There must have been a tremendous joy in converting isolated peoples to a bigger and easier picture of the world. Of all the religions none other is easier to pick on then Christianity, which is a shame because it has done so much good in the world, but it is quite fashionable to neglect that and stick to the events and side-effects that make a good excuse for some ritualistic self-flagellation.

Missionaries saw it as their destiny to bring the light to those still in darkness. A few centuries ago it was about 'saving souls' by making the ignorant see the joy in Christ, these days it's about 'saving souls' by showing them the jobs of consumerism. Missionaries did give way to merchants, which is no surprise, and the opening up of the New World yanked the Old World into what we have now: An interconnected world. While we are thoroughly globalised and access to information for all the blessed peoples of the lands is continuing, we want to know more and religions are not dying off: Many believe and want to believe more. In aggregate, in the eyes of a cunning alien species, we are still the lost tribe in the wilderness raising our arms up to pagans. In the eyes of the benevolent alien, regardless of what we already believe in, we're alone on our little planet waiting to be converted to something else.

What an alien race could convert us to is way beyond our comprehension. A tribe in Papua New Guinea, use to bowing down to crocodile gods and demonic dogs and weather fairies, would see very few parallels with Jesus and his Crew raising messiah-hell with the Jew Boys and the Occupying Roman Legions. Yet there was some magic, a lot of perseverance, breeding and more saving of souls: Those

Catholics sure knew how to increase their market share. In our modern times there is flow back: Some of the flock are ditching Christ for Buddha, or trusting themselves completely in science in holding all the cards. Last millennium, this millennium and next, religion will always be one of the things not to talk about at dinner parties (sex and politics being the other two). But an alien species doesn't have to make us change religions to convert us. They could just as easily jam all our media (television networks, internet, even all our PowerPoint presentations) with their own PowerPoint Presentation showing in pretty pictures and menacing bullet points the end of our solar system due to a defective sun, and we'd be worshipping and washing their slimy green feet in no time.

The goal of conversion is servitude. Be it new gods, apocalyptic threats, or promises of an afterlife, we are easy bait. In any case, it could be quite interesting to see how and why a conniving alien species would try to convert us. Are they as crazy as we were?

Prison Earth

In 1788 a British fleet of naval and convict ships reached their destination, what is now Sydney, and began one of the most amazing experiments known to mankind: White Australia began its life as a prison, most likely on a whim, by the powers that were in London, which was at the time building the mighty British Empire up to its zenith. The greatness of the British Empire relied on naval bases at convenient ports and junctures around the world (e.g. Malta, Singapore) to aid the free flow of commerce back to Britain. Why these masters of the seas decided on a convict settlement far, far away was simple: London was awash with criminals, they were rotting away in barges on the Thames and other crummy locations, and the idea of sending them to the other side of the world would act as a handsome deterrent to the thieves not yet convicted or contemplating a life of serial bread stealing and assorted crimes. Contrary to folklore, usually repeat offenders (not the bread thieves 'to feed my family, guv'nor' variant) were sent off to Botany Bay. The experiment continued and grew, with more convict settlements erected away from Sydney in places like Van Diemen's Land (Tasmania) and Brisbane.

To the resident population of Aboriginals it must have been very confusing for two reasons:

1. No European power had managed to settle anywhere on the Australian continent. Australia was the last continent to be settled, and the fact the British made it was all to do with timing – they were expanding at the time, had boat loads of convicts to jettison somewhere, and the vague eastern outline of New Holland (former name of Australia) as charted by Captain James Cook must have looked bizarre, yet still inviting, for the cause. Why a large tract of Australia was called New South Wales is baffling, so uncanny things seem to have been in abundance.

2. The white aliens set up a prison. Aboriginals are mostly nomadic, and differences were usually settled with a duel or a trial; painful, savage, and violent, their way. Importantly, a prison was not a concept they were familiar with. Even today, imprisoned Aboriginals have a high suicide rate; they see it as the end, rather as a brief stay courtesy of Her Majesty.

It's no surprise that Aboriginal Australians are still trying to come to grips with the modern world that washed up on their shores. Alcohol, new diseases and European mentality caused the Aboriginal people all sorts of calamities. For the convicts, it must have been bewildering to be sent to the far side of the known world, into an unknown land, to serve time for crimes for which one may never return. Many never did, they became modern day Australians, and seek revenge on the British by visiting London, drinking too much and vomiting where they see fit, probably on the very spot where their ancestor from six generations ago was picking pockets, the embodiment of Dickens's Artful Dodger.

As for the deterrent that Australia was meant to be, there is no evidence that it worked. Convicts who had served their time enjoyed settling this new wide land. The prison became a paradise. The end game is simple to understand though: Britain had another colony, and how it acquired them was rarely the sugar-coated tales from polished historical fairy tales.

So is it plausible that aliens would drop off their undesirables on the lovely blue planet?

Well, in a nutshell, why shouldn't it be? The assumption that all aliens are fun loving, gregarious, good natured, and beyond malevolence, is a typical naïve trait that has bitten countless earth civilisations in the behind numerous times. And, if ET has some bad apples in his sack, and a sense of humour, and finds earth a completely incomprehensible place on the far, far side of the galaxy, why not offload some undesirables there, after all, according to Dante, Hell is the impossibility of reason: the most ingenious of prisons. And Hell must be a universal threat.

Diplomatic solution: Get in on the act. In fact, expand the operation. Comply with the powers that prefer earth as a place for offenders, particularly galactic political offenders. Earth is so desperate for knowledge of what's out there, hosting a prison can only be a positive step.

Pirate Cove Earth

All pirates need a headquarters, somewhere out of the way, far from suspecting eyes, and where the native populace are none the wiser.

To wide-eyed earthlings, any swash-buckling alien waltzing down the gangway from a UFO pock-marked with laser beams or space debris, would be treated with the highest of respect. They would be feted like a demi-God, offered a permanent base by any nation wily enough to have a glimmer of geopolitical vision, and feel quite at ease dazzling their new docile friends with technology from light years away.

E:T. need not be Captain Blackbeard, or even Sir Francis Drake, plundering the seas and raiding Spanish ports, he/she/it could just be a rogue, even an individual seeking sanctuary. An elaborate cover could last for as long as required.

Diplomatic solution: If there are aliens, then there are pirate aliens. And then there will be alien law enforcement officers. The decision making on who to side with becomes tricky, so from the very beginning play innocent, yet be on the payroll of both parties.

The Bet's on Us

To the average earthling, the fact that we are not in regular contact with aliens yet are fed enough material to 'want to believe' something is out there, means there is a simple conclusion: They're out there but we're not ready, which means they're watching, which implies the investment in time and energy in surveillance must have an upside for them. When or how earth reaches this point, where the upside is delivered or leveraged to our observant alien friends, who knows. It might be a milestone we don't even know exists yet, but whatever it is, someone out there has a bet on us.

Diplomatic Solution: What does any good gambler do? Risk it all and raise the stakes! And why not? If an Alien Culture is betting on us coming good, we should be pro-active with our own space related developments and get busy. It's in our best interest to make sure that the returns of own endeavours will be so amazingly high that any observing aliens will want to get in on the action. Then we have contact and the game roles on! Impress then, seek their input and investment in us, and then they, the investor and the gambler as one, are hooked into the bet. They won't pull out for fear of losing their principle, and then they will want to invest more to leverage the investment off the scale. We should play on the nature of the gambler, on the galactic level.

A Virtual Experiment

If you have ever met someone who will talk you into (and in my experience, I met someone who wrote a book on it and set up his own stall at a New York Book Expo) the argument that alien intervention played a part in our evolution, and if you stare in their eyes long enough, you'll really start to believe that they're in fact the alien, so it must be true. Cringing experiences aside, there are other theories that end with the same point: We're just an experiment. Accept and scale up the concept and lamentation that we are someone else's experiment, in this humble dimension no doubt (maybe this is a sandbox dimension), we can extrapolate about our whimsical 'wondering about the Gods' because they, or one of them, is the chief designer; maybe God is a teenager-alien-games-designer sitting in his bedroom having a big laugh and impressing his game-designing friends, "Look what I invented! So far it's evolved up to 7 billion souls who have no idea what their purpose on their planet is for, but wait, I'm programming a cataclysmic apocalypse to see who survives and we can watch them ponder, panic and kill each other off. Cool, huh?"

We may even be a very well organised and monitored virtual experiment that is then hacked by giddy inter-galactic teenagers.

If we are an elaborate experiment that goes all the way to quantum mechanics and a horde of things our top boffins are slaving away to identify (like the Higgs boson), then all our attempts at finding the end of the maze may be disastrous: the designer can dissolve the game. He can pull the plug, start again, our bodies will collapse into a pile of atoms. The surface of earth would experience a tingling feeling as the combined electrical charge of atomising bodies and souls fizzles away. All that would be left to hear are the waves crashing on shores and the wind eroding the mountains – if they aren't part of the experiment.

Diplomatic Solution: Don't outshine the master, when you know a master exists. There are experiments where we push the limits of our own world (digging for the sub-particles that make up our world), yet at some stage we will face the morbid wall – there is no way out – but maybe another side (dimension). Of course we can play that as someone's creations they should be proud, and like Dolly the cloned sheep, we should be free to wander the rolling green pastures and be ever so thankful for our existence. This may explain religion, and reverence to Gods. Many simply believe that stuck in nature's chaos, it was the gods that positioned us here. We are alive thanks to the Gods, be it Zeus, the geeky alien game designer, or your idea of God. For atheists to prove that God is dead or doesn't exist, they have to first prove that we are not in the safety of a virtual experiment. Chew on that, heathens / dirty kuffars.

A Zoo

We haven't killed ourselves off yet, but we certainly have snuffed quite a few other species. Alien intervention that may save our souls may not have our souls in mind, after all a super brain alien soul would, sorry spiritually speaking, be mega spiritually in touch, a lot more than ours, and look down on us as we do things like bears, tigers, and penguins. Perhaps we are equal in the souls department, perhaps not. Perhaps ET is a zoo keeper. He makes visits, checks on us, observes what we're eating, where and what we're defecating (e.g. giving back to the *environment*), mindful if we start eating each other, in which case he may bestow wonderful technology on one side, or obliterate the other.

Not surprisingly, ET the Zoo Keeper charges exorbitantly to other Aliens to come and view the cute and furless bipeds, perhaps we're a lesser known and lesser exotic zoo; off the main highway, visited only by families lost in their warp speed family wagons.

Humans need zoos because it reminds us of the wild, and the captivity of animals soothes our own sense of captivity – for an alien race no matter how advanced they are and how far they can roam, their own sense of captivity in an expanding universe will be alleviated by our own captivity: We are trapped on earth, and though commercial space is rising, our few and feeble efforts to explore beyond earth have been run solely by our governments or billionaires.

Diplomatic Solution: An inmate and attraction of the zoo soon gains notoriety, and being unable to break out, it's the visitors who someday band together and demand its release. If ET the Zoo Keeper is indeed charging Aliens entry to this zoo, or conducting tours, or just keeping a watch over his stock (the talent), his customers will (hopefully) rally and demand that unless we are pure automata animalistic beings (like sharks), we be granted higher rights of sorts. On earth, the rise of animal rights may be a good sign that in the eyes of aliens, we're mature enough for rights too.

Cargo Cult Earthlings

This notion of salvation from above is prevalent in many cultures. A religion offering an enjoyable after-life is one form, the television Game Show and middle-class welfare are modern variations, but infinitely more interesting is the Cargo Cult.

It is possibly the strangest yet exotic phenomena observed in traditional (think: grass-skirt, topless dancing) cultures. From New Guinea to the Solomon Islands to Melanesia and the New Hebrides, many communities, separated by seas and their own individual languages, spontaneously took on the same type of observation and therefore bizarre belief: When white culture (and produce) would retreat from their islands, his cargo, notably Western produce, would be bequeathed to the tribes.

In a nutshell, and to paint an easy example, white colonialists and other forces came to remote places where supplies had to be shipped or flown in. To a local tribe, the sight of the whites clearing a runway, manning a radio, and waiting for a bird from the sky to deliver tinned foods and many other marvels that would seem to be the cream of some God in the Sky's crop, the whole process could easily be misinterpreted. The isolated tribes of the South Pacific missed out on the Romans, the Middle-Ages, the Industrial Revolution, but not spam, the old kind (tinned ham, for those of you who should be in bed by now) shipped around the world by the U.S. Military as they went at it with the tenacious Imperial Japanese forces in World War Two, in the South Pacific (if you're too young to know any of this, please study some history in your spare time. If you're an adult and you don't know this, you have a lot of reading to do). These tribes only saw the end product: Big noisy birds from the Gods (who else could possibly send them) and the delivery of all sorts of goodies. Imagine the supplies needed to fuel a battalion of soldiers, air-lifted to a remote island? It's no surprise then that some of these tribes, mostly after the white man had gone, enacted the arrival of the Gods and the raining down of food and marvels of the modern world through religious ceremonies. If you were around at the time you'd find rewarding employment as a witch doctor; supervising the clearing of an airfield, mimicking the 'talking to the gods' radio man (who has just informed the Battalion Commander that they're facing off with another bonsai charge), conducting the marching dances, wailing at the blue sky, and the sailing down to earth of booty. And your believers would probably be more captivated than you – it had happened before and it must happen again. The Gods did it for the previous generation, why not for us?

Any alien culture with a touch of anthropology in their culture would see earthlings' susceptibility to such frailties. Any visiting alien would be under stick orders to not feed the locals, nor present them with shiny gifts.

Alternatively, Aliens do not have to be burdened by maturity. They may be burdened by knowledge, and very apt at using it for their own advantage – enslaving a planet by their own beliefs. Of course the gifts of technology would have to be overwhelming, yet it's reasonable to say that one breed of Alien only has to play the Cargo Cult card on one breed of earthling: Be it religion, superpower, or rogue state.

Diplomatic Solution: Discipline is the key here. Whoever receive the gifts from above must have the discipline to understand they and we are not worthy of it, yet. However, for a handsome fee, I am sure they will come to an agreeable 'sharing' arrangement.

More alarmingly, Cargo Cult Earthlings culture may actually be ingrained already. There are no shortage of sects who are right now waiting for a mother ship to whisk them away to some paradise way out of our sun's gravitational pull. On a mass market level, there's no shortage of science fiction fans devouring tall tales where aliens meet and greet and empower lesser beings. Sometimes a sci-fi tale becomes mainstream, making the bridge with an old fashioned fairy tale where a handsome prince rescues a down and out, gorgeous, servant girl from a life of servitude.

Beads for Manhattan

According to history or folklore, almost one and the same in the digital age, the Dutch bought Manhattan from Native Americans for $24 worth of beads and trinkets. There is no solid evidence of this transaction, apart from a letter written by a Dutch merchant called Pieter Schagen in 1626. Writing to the directors of the West India Company, who had been granted ownership of New Netherland, Schagen claimed that the Dutch on the island of Manhattan 'have bought the island of Manhattes from the savages for a value of 60 guilders'. What supposedly changed hands and what that amount would be worth today, and what the value of Manhattan is worth (with or without the Twin Towers) is irrelevant. What we want to hear is a parable of how nasty capitalist Europeans swindled those poor decent Native Americans out of some prime real estate. Geopolitical swindling is evidence of history, otherwise all would be equal, borders would never shift, and we'd still be poking each other in the eyes with pointed sticks.

Is earth at risk from some well dressed Aliens dangling marvellous inventions before our wide eyes? The answer is firstly a robust 'No', because we (or those Muppets in power looking after us) wouldn't let it happen, unless of course we are naïve against all superior cultures. So, in short, it can happen, and more definitely, it will happen. An Alien presence on earth will lead to trade and ownership of something, not necessarily everything – save that for the hordes on Mars eyeing our blue jewel and everything we've got – but there is scope for a trade. 'Not being swindled' is a paranoia at the top of many culture's minds, and in any trade one plays the sheep, the other the wolf. Does anyone expect our first inter-galactic trade to be a windfall, and if it was profitable, who profits?

Diplomatic Solution: If Aliens do try a quick deal, or even a long drawn out bartering act, it doesn't hurt to ask for more. When facing the first offer, always look offended. Ratchet up the stakes. Pull some poker faces, keep the game going and make them sweat. In the end we will be swindled, so sell them a radioactive dump before a coral reef.

The Classic: The Trojan Horse

An alien Trojan Horse invasion hardly needs explanation, your puny earthling imagination is probably roaring to life and already protesting incongruously: But how could we possibly let benevolent looking and acting aliens land on our beautiful blue planet dressed in tuxedos and walking like harmless penguins suddenly assassinate our high ranking, democratically elected, photogenic politicians and United Nations officials greeting them, and then barbarically enslave us and suck all the water from the earth?

History: Who gave blankets with small pox to American Indians?

Diplomatic Solution: Bad Aliens have us in the palm of their hand, so being diplomatic may only be digging our own grave deeper. If they can pull the Trojan Horse trick on us, they will. Quit the appeasement and take up the pitch fork. Your planet needs you.

The Nutcases Beacon

On earth we have nutcases, specialists who take time out to scare anyone who is listening, of the apparent dangers of everything you have little or no interest in.

Apocalyptic doom and feel good motivations almost go in hand.

Some of these nutcases champion the communication with aliens. They make sound arguments by pointing to bits of evidence bobbing along on the flotsam of internet-junk crafted military secrets and suburbanised folklore.

If they're not proclaiming the world will end, they know someone who has telepathic conversations with aliens regarding Extraterrestrials governance. They may even elaborate on The Council of 8: the intelligent civilizations of the Pleiades, Orion, Sirius, Bootes, Alpha Centauri, Comsuli, Zeta, Reticuli, and Pouseti, who have graciously taken on the caretaker role of earth for the last million years. Apparently they have maintained Earth under 'protective quarantine' following an attempted 'invasion'. Holy cow. That was close.

Some Nutcases may not be so nuts, some want the governments of the world to disclose the secret contacts and covert diplomacy already going on between aliens and who ever on earth has managed to wrangle their way into the negotiator's seat.

If at its worst the Nutcases are all wrong, they may pose a danger to any alien pondering popping down and saying hello and doing whatever they set out to do; They may scan the world's media and dig deep enough and find nutcases painting a sordid and distorted picture of the true reality.

If only a small fraction of the Nutcases are ever proved right, they may just have been lucky in predicting what kind of alien would ever choose to visit and why. Ten points for creativity, ingenuity and courage.

If a very, very, few Nutcases (a very, very, few because if even a very few Nutcases were ever right is not worth contemplating) are right, have had contact with weird and wonderful aliens, would they not profit from it, other than creating scam organisations to entrap suckers into weekend meditation camps? If you had a direct telepathic line to Martians, and even if you were a die-hard Marxist, at some point you would leverage this gift into a form of power. When an 'Aliens Are Amongst Us' Nutcase emerges that turns their vision and personal hotline to a 'key invading alien decision maker' into an Intergalactic Entrepreneurial Enterprise that makes them trillions, not billions, then you must bow down to them and hand over your business card, because the Nutcase will now be our esteemed and revered Diplomat to Aliens.

Diplomatic Solution: Absolutely none. If one of the true Nutcases are ever right, be prepared to eat your hat.

Very Interesting or Plain Oddity Earth

Would earth be seen as strange or weird? We inadvertently categorise people (weird friends, nauseatingly weird family, whacko colleagues, and other races) into these categories, so aliens may not be that different. Peruse these two hypothetical scenarios:

Number One. On the planet Splatter, very, very, very far away, is a gas station for refuelling your space craft. Sometimes, those who pass through Splatter, musing on how 'everything that can be discovered, has been discovered, and life, though for some be it eternal, is really quite boring' ask the gas station staff, a very friendly breed of general (to the universe) inter-galactic peasant, the following: "Say, is there anything remotely interesting for my amazing superior intellect, around here?"

Splatter Inter-Galactic Peasant 'A' looks the visitor up and down, and not too curious of where the visitor comes from, what they're doing out so far in the boondocks of this galaxy, and where they're going, then turns to Splatter Inter-Galactic Peasant 'B', and emits a long, drawn out chortle, that Splatter Inter-Galactic Peasant 'B' raucously crushes by leering at and daring the visitor, "If you want to see something funny, though some say more horrible than funny, that's not too far away, we'll even pack a picnic hamper for you because you won't stay there that long and all the other visitors there are back here for dinner, try earth."

Number Two. In the other direction to that of the planet Splatter, very, very, very far away, is a planet called Grey, because it is eternally grey. The beings there are somewhat advanced and astonished every single time some strange craft visits their grey world and seems to light it up a bit. There is conjecture whether they are really alone as they feel. One day the elites of Grey detect, because they're pro-active on this subject, a spike of communication from a planet very, very, very far away, that we call Earth. The wise inhabitants of Grey waste no time in handing the hat around, tooling a craft for the mission, and fare welling their intrepid astronauts. The journey may take ten or a thousand years, and until the people of Grey receive a report back about Earth, they will hold Earth in a very, very, high regard.

Diplomatic Solution: From a diplomatic point of view, and if you believe in destiny, whether we are interesting or an oddity is way beyond our control, but the outcomes are very important. Each country's politicians and media always seem to paint their respective lands as if though not exactly the centre of the world stage, it's at least very, very close to it. The challenge for any aspiring Diplomat to Aliens is to brand earth above how visitors may (sneeringly) view it.

Also remember that on an earth social level, when it comes to 'oddities', one is considered 'eccentric' if they are financially comfortable or wealthy (regardless if they made their money from the application of their eccentricity), or just 'weird' if they're poor and lower-middle-class. Society is cruel. The depths of space will be crueller.

The Sticks to Beat Us With

Quite often in life it's those that love us that hurt us the most. On the topic of life, as in life other than our collective lives, we could probe Nietzsche and a horde of other sobering philosophers to the moment when our egos are proved right and some aliens out there really do think of us as much as we think of us. It will be a psychological and philosophical field day. People will queue for miles just to get a quarter hour slot with their local psychoanalyst, to help conquer what alien contact means to *them*.

Our weakness, for contact to mean something, even something meaningful, is what any aspiring alien can use to beat us with. They know what they want out of the contact and precisely how to get what they want, plus create some frivolity; which is the fabric of life and makes the space-time continuum less boring, in order to control us. How they control us very much depends on who they are and at what level of evolutionary loveliness or nastiness they have reached.

Because the Universe is supposedly accelerating out to nowhere and infinite, there are innumerable types of aliens out there. To explain them in great detail would involve removing your humble brain and implanting it into something more powerful. So make things easier, we can divide Aliens Out There into two types:

The Thugs. Yes, thugs from outta space. They come to our planet like in some block buster Hollywood movie and raise hell. They have the ray guns, the lasers, the shape-shifting capability, and they love oppressing the weak. The stick they beat us with is superior technology. Earth is no stranger to one culture snuffing the other thanks to superior technology, and the Thugs spare no mercy in subjugating us helpless earthlings. In the end we'll be slaves or fertiliser, end of story, unless a roguish action hero or a home grown bacteria saves the day.

The Sentient Beings. They are so far advanced they hardly remember where or what sludge they crawled out of so many billions of years ago. They're so 'out there' they can't even remember the purpose of their big trip over this way into the Milky Way. But they arrive in some shape and have already studied us, and not entirely sure why, they simply must have something over us. There doesn't need to be a rationale, earth is no stranger to 'holier than thou' cultures converting 'lesser' cultures to religions that seemed 'shit hot' or 'super cool' at the time. Many a heads have rolled over a preference to un-provable Gods. And so it will be with the sneaky Sentient Beings: They're here to change our will on some agenda, and not wishing to draw their light sabres from their scabbards nor get them blood splattered, will resort to other milder methods to make us tow their line. Conversion (as discussed previously) is the goal and all the Sentient Beings have to do is create some event that eclipses all we have come to expect from our own home grown religions and apocalyptic predictions. Once we see something amazing, it's in our nature to strive to find a complete understanding of why it happened, and as a bonus, somehow blame ourselves for it. For the Sentient Beings, far superior in forms of guilt, violence and taste than the humble Thugs, their act of oppression is the miraculous: Create a new sun in our solar system (as per 2010, the sequel to 2001: A Space Odyssey), melt the Arctic Ice Caps, throw a cloud of opaque gas between us and our own sun, bring back the dinosaurs, or even send down a messiah. Whatever happens, we'll (or not you and I, but those uncontrollable masses) be there to fall to our feet.

Beware the light that guides you may blind you, and that the to stick to guide us by, beats us as well.

It's Not About Us

The stage is set. A mother ship descends. The world's leaders and public relations spinners are there, ready to greet what we know will be a very advanced and sage species who look a bit funny, have travelled 20,000 light years (at half the speed of light), and are probably gagging with claustrophobia to go for a brisk walk outside their crammed ship. So, they land, they walk the red carpet carrying a harpoon, they look around, and say, "What the fuck is wrong with you humanoids? We are here for the whale hunting season. Take us to the nearest and most exotic pod! I'm hungry for some sperm whale! I haven't had some raw whale blubber in 20,000 earth years."

They're here for anything but us. In terms of inter-galactic intelligence in the Milky Way, we may be a few steps below average. We may be plain boring on many levels. What may be really exciting about earth is what's around us, what's overlooked, what's underfoot, and what we've made of it. This shouldn't be much of a surprise (after the initial let-down) because earth does have bio-diversity, and that may be of more value than our egotistic selves.

Diplomatic Solution: If you are a free thinker, probably right wing leaning, and have had to swallow the waffle from hard core environmentalists, it's easy to understand the natural recoil and repulsion at anything to do with the environmental movement. Sadly for the environmental movement, and here's the gag line – for the environment – much of the early environmental movement seems to have evolved from left leaning, vehemently anti-nuclear weapon, and therefore anti-nuclear power, long-haired anti-capitalist hippy types. Now that the environmental movement has swum upstream and gone mainstream, political, and if elected too far into power may re-invent fascism for their own purposes, they are a force, untried and unpredictable from the fringe (the Nazis and Khmer Rouge were from the fringe), that must be reckoned with. But peel away the noises they make to get our attention and there is an element of reality: At some point the environment needs protection. Why it needs protection is obvious enough, and as an added bonus, some higher culture may value it as well. An alien species may even thank us for saving our planet's biodiversity, because on their planet they squandered it and have since then roamed the cosmos for a lost Eden: A new world on which to start again, atone old environmental sins. And yes, they'd wipe us out just to have a vacant earth and hence a chance to feel better about themselves.

World War Three Denial

The next war could be the last, or World War Four may be fought with pointed sticks between mutated off-spring of post-apocalyptic earthlings. However, World War Three doesn't have to be a nuclear Armageddon; the decline of the United States rubbing noses with the apparent rising Chinese Empire (under the dubious branding of the hammer and the sickle) can lead to a hi-tech war, albeit with minimal nuclear reprisals, and hopefully just a few tactical nuclear strikes. Using small scale nuclear weapons on the battle-field (e.g. attacking ground forces or even tightly grouped fleets) will not lead to a devastating nuclear winter. However, when cold wars get hot, the inevitable threat remains: Shooting between ships with high speed missiles can escalate to nuclear tipped thrusts on enemy forces that will lead to nuclear strikes on bases. Military bases aren't conveniently far away from civilians, in fact it makes sense to have brothels as close as possible to bases. If wars begin to creep into a terminal nuclear phase, then our alien friends may decide to step in.

In the old days when nuclear arsenals were grouped in silos or riding on long range bombers from fixed, interfering with earthlings' genocide tendencies was much easier. Now nuclear weapons are in silos, on long range bombers, at bases, in submarines designed to lurk, aboard aircraft carriers to be loaded on bombers, on missile launching trucks, in transit, and if you believe the early 21st century hysteria about terrorism, in suitcases. White terrorists are hard to control (God can always step in, but where is he when terrorists are racing against the clock for a date with 72 virgins?) but the command and control systems of nuclear-armed powers are prone to a specific weakness: Satellites.

Satellites of Love

Satellites are the unsung umbilical cord we have with space. Recent space exploration politics has split into two parties. First are those, like the Americans, willing to pay to push man further (and stoically holding out against nations' budget cuts and financial crisis) because it is imperative that earthlings spread beyond our comfort zone, and still send up satellites. Next are the Europeans and patient believers in technology, their space efforts lean more towards gadgets that draw in more data about how the world and the galaxy around us works. More satellites, wonderment, questions.

Earth will always push out with satellites like a torch in a mine because spacecraft are cheaper than earth-replacements: The space craft that have the technological ability to ferry humans for a long, long time to their destination, and then back home.

For the love of satellites the honeymoon is over: To wave the 'FUCK. OFF.' flag on an emerging towering height, China and the United States have both bagged a satellite with missiles (usually a defunct satellite of their own (to date)), and yet the old-school Soviet Union had already tested several anti-satellite weapons.

Game up? Spies in the spy, and all satellites, are fair game?

Just a few exploding satellites pose an even greater problem – already there are 20,000 pieces of space debris below 10cm whizzing by. More debris is incalculable. You can even buy shares in a company that tracks space debris with a laser, I have. A speck of debris can collide with a satellite with an impact speed of over 40,000 kilometres per hour.

A grand alien gift would be the technological means to clean up space debris, something environmentalists should ponder funding for, but the hard reality is that earth will have to overcome its first space problem, alone and dignified, or just built harder-to-destroy satellites.

The Space Arms Race is already on. There are people and the military drumming up treaties to keep space neutral for us and extra-terrestrials. So how long one of our own rules is broken in the name of self-preservation?

The end game in a space war in earth orbit can only be a satellite so chunky and thick that it simply bashes opposing satellites out of the way, or satellite-hunting-satellites like itself, with little chivalry from the days of jousting. The Cold war was a fertile innovative field to develop weapons to slap the other guy's weapons, space is a logical elevation.

Successive world wars have pushed technology on to the masses, first by killing them, then servicing them, and space won't be much different.

Yet there is nothing to fear. Who controls space, in the immediate case low orbit to geosynchronous orbit, has control over spying, navigation, communications, and the best weather reports. Satellite technology will become more competitive than ever, and if ever an alien culture wants it over us, they'll still have the means to tear our flimsy little birds into pieces.

Intergalactic Economics

verses Us

It is not from the benevolence of the butcher, the brewer, or the baker that we expect our dinner, but from their regard to their own interest.

Adam Smith, The Wealth of Nations

The First Trade

Before we surf the concepts of earth shooting up in intergalactic stature and wheeling and dealing with a myriad of alien cultures spread out over catchy-named star systems inhabited by both benevolent and cunningly greedy fellow traders, as if earth were like some under-weight developing country punching above its weight and then making a killing out of globalisation, think of the first meaningful trade that might actually come our way.

As probed previously, an Alien would value unique and transferable items from earth. No alien would come here to buy gold (unless to manipulate our economies) or real estate (unless they wanted to establish a physical presence) or stocks (unless they wanted to leverage their investment against us).

Earth money is relevant to earth, has no relevance outside of humanity's spread, so what is transferrable with an alien currency?

Following the rules of supply and demand, inspect the visiting aliens' shopping lists: Artefacts, art, memorabilia, specimens, information, friendship, a memento.

And what do we get in exchange? If not, then a handful of alien currency we can use with the next visitors. As in many first trades, the advanced civilisation was centuries ahead of the locals. Think of all the agreements where a tribe's chief fumbles with a pencil across a foreign contract and remove whole islands or peninsular from his world. Trinkets, mirrors and nails were popular trades for early explorers. The worst case is we end up a visiting alien's equivalent of fridge magnet promoting the wonders of their tourist hot spots. Come again.

The Better Trades

After the initial ceremonial first trades comes the realisation that "we're wasting each others' time and worthless currencies" and then the thrusts for what is of real value.

Now, whatever is scarce become valuable (both ways), and out of the initial confusion and fanfare some economic theories will displace others. Yet the problem still remains, what can earth offer an alien culture other than saleable parts of our own culture, or what little reserve of alien currency we've amassed; most would be pilfered and secreted away by our untouchable financial elites anyway.

There will be minimal demand for precious metals because any craft that got this far will know how to repair itself while getting here and returning. A whole range of hard commodities are likewise excluded because minerals can be found in asteroids and many of our tradable objects would be completely worthless to an alien; toilets, toilet brushes, toilet paper, tooth brushes, tooth paste, televisions, time-share apartments... Anything else beginning with T?

However, some items are 'collectible's but not tradable. We do however have an abundance of objects that can be sold and transferred quite easily, yet even art, historical fragments and information (printed and digital) are possibly valuable but not enough, so entrepreneurial earthlings will step ahead to the next level.

The Service Agreement

Read up on any dirt poor backward nation that had the leadership with the moral fibre to say "We will do better" and you'll see that their early years were spent doing the shit work few other equally shittier nations bothered with.

While earth can't really manufacture cheap goods for an alien culture thanks to time and distance, earth can offer a service to a visiting Alien Culture. Be it washing their Star Cruisers, shampooing their hair, exfoliating their skin, fornicating for their voyeurs, who knows.

All we do know is that trade on earth is mature relative to earth. Peace is not so mature but getting there, science is forever pushing ahead and then sometimes sideways or backwards (think of scientific fads full of hot air), religion will always be religion, yet commerce is a beast unto itself.

Learn and Imitate

The lessons from nations that changed their destiny is that they performed the grunt work not just out of dedication to work or some other magical social theory, but because they wanted to learn and profit from their masters. Modern China owes it modern military might to the formative years when they built their first Western inspired, designed and even owned (until shuffled out by the Communist Party) factories.

Who on earth scales a simple service agreement with visiting aliens to something larger will be gaining an insight and a stepping stone to the stars.

The Merchants

When earth is part of an intergalactic economy it will be because earthlings have built on their exposure to alien culture, profited from a transfer of technology, and taken the initiative to fill a gap missing the universe. Ultimately, budding capitalists may do more for the preservation of humans and earth by forging trade relationships with yet to be met alien cultures.

This intergalactic capital ethos, though at odds with what might actually exist and evolve out there, is the most pro-active method to get earthlings organised and efficient at arming and kitting themselves with alien equipment. No matter how we portray ourselves or who is in power on earth, we will be 'aliens' with funny ways, but what binds cultures from across un-charted seas and soon to be chartered space will be a form of money – not the money many associate with greed – but a form of money that recognises reward for effort and that is transferrable.

So, socialists, you won't get us to the stars.

They Made Contact and Asked Us Questions

Diplomacy: the art of restraining power.

Henry A. Kissinger

Contact! With Who?

Some international bodies have drafted protocols on how to handle contact with the Big A – Aliens.

These volunteer efforts are a start, and maybe your tax dollars fund government and military dreamers to get 'creative' on a totally unpredictable scenario. Yet what happens if aliens do arrive depends largely on who they create a dialogue with first.

And here's where it gets tricky – Do they initiate contact with who they want, or do they land and we by default direct them to who we think is up for the job.

In either situation, there's pros and cons about any of the main groups we'd expect to do contact. Who should we prefer do our talking for us?

The Government, Guv'nor.

If you're the pro-active type, can you sincerely trust a government to do your talking for you, even if you gaily voted them in? Your tax pays them to do your talking for you, and as a bonus impose on you things you've never, ever talked to them about at all. Most of the time you have no choice what they're talking about so you're use to them misrepresenting you. A day without your government mishandling something would be like a day without light: You would sense something is very wrong and troubling.

If they're doing the first-contact with aliens, at the very least your expectation for a successful outcome is already low. Stay down there. Right now, a government employee (on flexi-time (working a half day), job-sharing with someone else working half of a half day) is tinkering the fine print on a document that stipulates the diplomatic legalities binding our culture to an alien culture, only for the next 1,000 years. On the plus side, they may be slow and cumbersome, but that might be the multi-layered buffer needed between aliens and the common man.

At the Commander-in-Chief level of Government, when someone is running the government and they are (hopefully, gulp) democratically elected from a population that is not dumb as mutton, they do by default have the mandate to be the lead diplomat with aliens. After all, we voted them in? But who is the we? Is the President of the United States more important than the leader of China or Russia? If aliens were in direct contact with one, and one of the others knew about it, then it would be in their best interest to expose the flaw: We on earth are not one (waning or rising) superpower, we are many.

Scientists / Boffins / Geeks

Can you trust in scientists, boffins and geeks to do your Exoplanet Risk Management for you. Yes, the scientists have the models, the software for all eventualities, and the process of peer review, to enable hard-facts, brain-draining, super-analytical, decision making. These masters of the elements have created all the synthetic things in our lives (plastic, food additives, the formula in the database behind the online dating website that allowed you to be automatically matched with 'the true one' for just a 'fling' that ended with bitter taste in your mouth), so why stop them now? The only problem however, is that rational as they are, an alien interaction may be way out of their best rational calculations. What are we to do then, if what an alien asks is completely way over their heads and incomprehensible? What do they say? In that case, call in the clowns to do the talking. On that note...

The United Nations

There exists in Vienna, the United Nations Office for Outer Space Affairs (UNOOSA), and after several international newspapers reported that an astrophysicist was appointed by UNOOSA to be Earth's first extraterrestrial spokesperson, the United Nations made a firm denial. Not a good start, in any sense, to trust the United Nations to stretch their agile and acute minds to diplomacy with an alien species. They probably should have someone, publically, on the record, squirreling away on what to do in any alien-to-earth eventuality. If it's a question of money, how can one more wage (with all the frills and benefits) of a bureaucrat be a problem? The sad reality is that the United Nations is a nice concept, but the people in it are not perfect, or accountable, just a bit more qualified in areas of diplomacy than the average government. But, it is a figurehead, and a brand, that we do accept as speaking for our respective countries, so why not our planet.

The Bankers (that Sold the World)

Who would trust that a well connected private entity, like a bank, should be the first port of call for any visiting alien? The East India Company was an English joint-stock company formed initially to create trade in the East Indies. Therefore, to a merchant in India and China, their view of the west was formed by their relationship with a company, not a government or a people. Why should inter-planetary contact be any different? If aliens did descend on Wall Street or the Square Mile or in Frankfurt, Paris, Beijing or Tokyo or any other financial hub, don't panic, they're just coming for a loan, or some other commercial activity. They may want to invest in earth, or buy it, pump it, dump it, and we'll be some inter-galactic toxic sub-prime loan – but it'd be better than being alone.

A commercial minded contact is almost inevitable because like it or not, the language of money on our planet is universal, and money (in this case some inter-galactic currency) must also be ultimately universal. What shape would this money take: Information. And what is this information: You'll have to buy it to find out.

Oh, dear God!

Can humanity trust the religious leaders, or the leaders of the most populous, or popular, religions, to think benevolently of all of Earth's peoples, creatures and deities, when making both casual and serious chit chat with a visiting alien power? This is probably the most morally appealing decision because we outsource moral imploring to our moral leaders, in turn trusting in the actions or lack of action of our gods. Also, praying is a two-way communication: the gods are tuned in, they know the path. You get struck by lightning, cured of all of your weird sexually transmitted diseases, live a reasonable happy and non-poor life, or you don't.

So what if aliens want to talk directly to the world's religious leaders? If all religions, and therefore religious leaders form a scrum and have it out with whatever arrives before them from another planet (another realm), it'll seem quite moronic, tragic, colourful, but entertaining to watch on television, and if that's what the believers of the world want (and there are more believers (though of them being a virtual pet, no-one has asked that) than non-believers (who wouldn't be at all surprised to be supervised in an alien's virtual experiment)) and what an alien wants, then that's what we'll get.

However, if an alien bee-lines for a particular religious group, then all the others will have a fit, and if they don't decide to convert to the winning religion, they'll have a nice little war about it too.

The nagging answers to the nagging question of why aliens would assume to make contact first and foremost with any religious element are: Their gods are angry with them, they have very deep spiritual questions, they've come to convert us, or they know that control over earthlings is through control over earth's religions.

The Military

They are entrusted with your security, and they usually have the best technology, so they have a definite advantage. Yet against a superior alien race, the military have little to say, or do. After all, their start of the art weaponry amounts to no more than to flimsy darts when against formidable, advanced, cross-galaxy and maybe even multi-dimension battle tested, ray guns. Or the aliens have weapons we can't imagine, but maybe a hack sci-fi writer has craftily speculated, but being a hack, his or her work never reaches the wider public and we have no idea what we're in for. Neither do the military: Our modern armies take decades to shift stance from Cold War to War on Terrorism. By the time most modern forces are equipped to hunt fanatics in caves, the tide will turn and it will be the age of the pocket-battleship-satellite.

Unknown-unknowns is the catch word yet an alien contact, if they're up to nastiness, is unknown-unknown-unknown. Play that out in a simulation, test that in a war game, and then release a report about it to the public: Any race that makes it here can pretty much do what they want with us. History offers a treasure trove of examples, and the Spanish Conquistador are a shining example: With their European diseases sometimes preceding them, the local populace, often struggling against new and nasty epidemics, was easy to decimate.

If aliens are on their best behaviour and instigate contact with the military, then we can assume that it's the discipline and secrecy of the military that they value. Perhaps the shock of alien contact upon our societies is something that only our military can contain.

The (gulp) Prophet (sigh)

The Prophet, I hear you asking? What is a Prophet these days anyway? Well, to be a profitable prophet, you need media appeal, charisma, and funding. You also need to connect like the slimiest politician and vaporise your detractors like the best of the Roman Emperors. To command from the towering heights in spiritual matters, you must outshine Jesus, Buddha and Mohammed. Being the Prophet that talks to visiting aliens is a very hard task indeed. And where do we find this prophet? They could very well be a Nutcase (as discussed earlier) or they could be the right politician, scientist or general in the right place at the right time to make the right round of sound-bytes that summarises 'actual alien contact' for the awe-struck masses wired into CNN or Twitter. Someone can easily step in the limelight and steal a good show with a few crafty one-liners.

Competition will be tough, but it is history in the making, and who in a position of power would want to miss out?

The other avenue for the Prophet is the contestant that survives the ordeal and is ordained as the 'one' to do the talking with 'the Aliens'. Reality television shows, like their game show predecessors, filter from the 'chosen few' the 'chosen one', almost too predictability. If there are reality television shows for talentless artists, sociopaths, models and porn stars, then it's no great leap of the imagination to have a global show to find out who should be, as voted by esteemed judges (for a nominal fee) and the public, 'Our Diplomat to the Aliens!', and be showered with all sorts of adverting-backed valuables. If you think the author outlays this weird scenario to make up word count and fatten by a miserly one paragraph this text, then you are sadly mistaken. Creative ideas are not isolated. If the author dreams it, then there must be some TV producers meeting up in Cannes, scoffing down champagne and mulling over the same scenario, imagining how many billions would watch the franchised shows, how many entrants there would be, and what consumer items could be advertised to beef up the scripted entertainment and their wallets.

Answer Some Basic Questions

"No, you ask first."

Any one of the previous possibilities opens up wounds on many levels, and any choice (if there is a choice) triggers our new alien friends to ask some basic questions, and then finer questions, depending on who they're actually dealing with.

In any meeting of minds, as in interviews, friendly innocuous questions are potential probes for weaknesses. But some questions are ordinary, easy to answer, and still open to interpretation. We shall expect aliens to ask questions, and because they have the upper hand, they'll know what to ask, whereas earthlings will have a vague idea of what to ask except for the obvious: Where are you from, do you have ice cream there? A checklist of what to ask has been compiled for your ruthless examination further on.

Some basic questions from them will be to clear any confusion, and we should have some answers ready. Expect whoever is in charge of answering to prudent aliens to squirm over the following:

Earthlings, When Do You Stop Killing Each Other?

This is the opener for any earth-to-alien conversation. It neatly sets the stage and lowers us to some primate level – so beware – thump your fists on your chest or breasts and looked offended. By the way, it's none of their business when we stop killing each other.

What's their track record? What's their planet's strife-torn body-count in comparison to their population? Let's compare before we answer with the following: When we have abundance of food, energy and living space. Next.

At What Point Will Your Population Meet Environmental Sustainability?

Another typical opener. But, a tough one to tackle. China is a very brave and courageous country to maintain a one-child policy, genetically modified foods (though they weather bad PR and sometimes results) are increasing crop yield, and if it hasn't happened already, the number of obese people will outnumber starving people. Good question, and the answer is very simple: When the rule of law is enforced across all lands to abolish corruption and make fair and open trade more possible. To do that earthlings need something to believe in, so please alien visitors, share the spoils of the universe.

Do You Fancy Space Travel?

Yes. Some of us will sacrifice our first born for a whiff of space travel.

With any 'open' contact with aliens, and their offer to let some of us come for a ride, the more people who can partake the better. The opening of our eyes to space will do more good than a thousand painful reality television shows meant to explore our inner, nauseating selves.

Can I Buy Anything on Earth?

Yes! Establishing a trading link is probably the best form of communication. Forget diplomatic niceties, let's barter over the price of objects unique to earth (like, say, a toilet) with aliens from far, far away, who have never seen a toilet like ours before.

The Internet is Confusing Us

Their initial question will be a bit more arduous: Our onboard artificial intelligence has trawled through all the user profiles on Facebook, all the porn on the internet, read all the blogs and Twitter comments, and digested all digital content. We're still confused. We are pretty flat out processing all the data added to the internet, every second. Are we missing something?

Very tough to answer because the internet is not filtered, it is not like a traditional encyclopaedia, nor is it static enough to pin-point at any given time what all that data actually amounts to. The best answer is, "You tell us what it is."

Howdy, Partner

Partnering with "one" when there are no others to compare it with, other than our own limited history, is fraught with peril. A visiting partner-seeking alien will argue, "Join my wining team because out there are some bad ass aliens. Please sign here. Join our crew!"

And as a token of our participation they'll pay us with interesting barrels of a radioactive material.

Whatever deal is proffered, history shows, that we're very unlikely to profit in the first instance.

Only the Aliens Know

While contingency plans are made at all levels, it's most likely up to the visitor that decides who among the hosts to talk too, all dependent on their needs. If an alien culture has invested money and time getting here, a further small investment of active study of our culture will give them a firm idea of who to talk to first and why. And if aliens zoom down straight to the jungles of Africa and start by talking to the apes, we'll know we're in some deep shit.

They Leverage the Digital Age

We are more connected than ever before, more educated, and hungry for knowledge. We also recognise that no one voice can ever represent us. The digital age has democratised information, for good and for bad, and this communication is a two-way street, unless your government is paranoid and censors your internet.

While we will bemoan that not anyone should be the fulcrum which leverages all our voices with an alien culture, we have to accept that an alien culture, millions if not billions of years ahead of our own, has probably mastered our primitive digital technology, and can at a whim mass communicate with us, without us knowing about it. All an alien culture has to do is weasel into our communication network and spam us, coax us into conversation, and most importantly, interact with us, in order to extract what they need, to develop what we need.

As one can poke someone on Facebook, an Alien culture can mass poke humanity.

Diplomacy: Social Networks vs. News Networks

Alien Contact will be eclipsed by Alien Diplomacy, yet we trust our (if you're lucky) democratically elected governments to fill the diplomatic chair with competent people to do our talking and then we sit back and let the poker-faced games begin.

Wars have been waged over what seems trifle causes; World War One presenting a prime example if you care to sift through the historical build up and causes, where things obviously got out of hand leading to the organised murder of generations of young men in their prime. The outcomes was that a whole generation of women were without prospective partners, and a horde of children were without fathers. Alternatively, if diplomacy works between visiting aliens and our robust leaders, we praise ourselves for voting in our leaders. If diplomacy doesn't, the maddest and most determined of us reaches for a sniper rifle, while the rest moan and bleat about ineptitude, conspiracy or lack of justice.

In the pre-internet, mass-communication, analogue era of mass media the news networks had total control over information feedback: If there was credible alien contact in that period we wouldn't know about it, because a few key editors could block the syndication of a real page turner or ratings grabber that could lead to massive social upheaval. All the end consumer was left with was X-Files (a popular television series) and a few documentaries that managed to bubble up from alternate scenes into mainstream.

Thankfully, with all its warts and mundane media mashes, the internet is here to stay, so if something credible does happen it can spread as a virus and infect our minds, providing of course we aren't in suspended awe at some YouTube Stupidity Stunt Gone Viral (proving humanity is not as smart as we wished it could be).

An alien culture knows that feedback with billions of connected individuals is not accomplished by dealing with elected leaders' chosen diplomats and media monopolies, and that the true nature of alien diplomacy and its impact on earth should not be entrusted to a few elites who see no difference between commercial content and benevolent propaganda. An alien will prefer an open network as a fair alternative to a top-down hierarchy; a hierarchy that hasn't had any major success with alien contact yet. Aliens will see the value in Facebook (which is now as much an embedded utility as Google) for global feedback, and even the business focussed social media website LinkedIn. And as the internet was designed to withstand a nuclear attack (again, at your leisure, sift through the history behind the internet), it is resilient against censorship in most countries.

At the time of writing, a social network like Facebook has 800 million users. It may represent an instantaneous means to mass communicate with 10% of the world's population. However, not all Facebook users can be replied on to correctly interpret a message from the stars; most are awestruck by the common Hollywood stars' carefully crafted Twitter rants and what the gossip industry feeds people in order to ramp up fervour for the next vehicle for a star; a movie, a song or album, maybe even a book. The downside of social media is that it relied on herd mentality to gain a critical mass to sustain itself, and what does the herd do next? Cannibalise itself ? Facebook has potential, but there is something with much more appeal and connectivity: ET won't phone home, he'll text you.

Text Me

Mobile phone networks function (for all intents and purpose let's just jump over volumes of technical jargon about GSM, 3G, 4G etc and say...) because the data whizzes through the air: Ideal for a forced transmission.

For a forthright alien that requires immediate access to earth, they'd be extremely efficient if they layered earth orbit with some communication drones that in staggered (so as not to create a jam) sets commenced contact backed up by something visible. You get a text message that says, "Hello Dave. We are aliens and we real. We're making contact. If you don't believe in us, at high noon look out your window and you'll see one of our craft doing figure eight patterns over your capital at four times the speed of sound."

From that point, the 6 billion mobile phone subscribers can then quiz the alien visitor with whatever comes to mind. The beauty of text messaging is that the recipient can hopefully read and converse and is therefore not that dumb, and one message in one language can be used as the meta language of all translations. Unlike social media movement, the communication is one-on-one.

A 'mass alien texting' is probably the most 'open source' or 'crowd/swarm' inspired method for communication between them and us. After tedious questions and answers (answered thanks to some all knowing alien brain residing in an alien mother ship that maintains a vigil against attack from earth mobile phone carriers and their hedge fund owners) there would be some common ground established, the beginning of a bridge, and a sense of purpose. The mass-communicative aliens would then be able to probe and execute what they're after: How would humans like to be remembered before they're exterminated, or how deeply do humans wish to explore space, and a portion of their day and wealth they are willing to sacrifice for space exploration? At the moment, thanks to our top-down-hierarchy, the individual has little input on how a slice of their tax could be used to really inspire their offspring.

Sooner or later, mass communication forms a bedrock on which humanity comes to worship the messiah from the stars. The outcome is that humanity permitted its own destiny, and our elected leaders can sleep in peace, until they're ousted by shaggy haired, dog-like, extraterrestrials from the planet Melmac.

What if Science Fiction
is Right?

Your powers are weak, old man.

Darth Vader

Welcome Storm Troopers, tea or coffee?

It's irritating enough that entertainment is configured for consumption by the masses, what's more painful to swallow for the science fiction aficionado is that popular science fiction relies on the structure of populist fairy tales told long, long ago, not in a galaxy far, far, away, but around the campfire, by our ancestors, as they used their molars to crush bones for the nutritious marrow. All good stories use easily recognisable communal reference points and characters, which serves as junctures in the narrative for the audience to burp, scratch their arses, and nod in unison.

But, like it or love it, in the time we are allocated to entertain ourselves, we need entertainment that is mass produced and therefore mass digestible, because it gives us something to talk about.

Now when daring to venture on the subject of aliens coming to earth with a useful agenda (vaporising us with ray guns is not an agenda; perhaps a jolly sport), one of the first, almost primal instincts is to fear the worst. All fictional aliens seem to have suspect motives – and who can blame them, we must be easy to fool, *and* hunt down as our two skinny legs propel us through suburbia or jungle.

A real point of concern though, is the strange probability that we might meet our sci-fi masters of evil and galactic domination. They might actually exist. They might have invaded the dreams of science fiction novelists, script-writers, and producers and said, "Here's a sketch of me on a good day, put me on your puny two dimensional screens and make me look lean, mean and dangerous. If I'm unhappy with your work, I'll subtly increase the temperature of your blue planet by 1 degree every decade until your children's children with be boiled alive! There! Now you're scared!"

The probability of meeting characters from science fiction is actually higher rather than lower; we are only of value to alien species that value what we value. Good and evil exists, so do laser guns, worm holes, and thanks to the supposedly infinite nature of the universe, if we're capable of imagining something it should rightfully exist, either in the past, the now, or the future, but in a galaxy far, far away.

So what happens if we meet our worst fictional fears, and what are the chances that it will actually happen? Well there's one way to determine the chance of bad ass aliens coming to earth, and that's to see how they scored at the Box Office. Think of the most famous sci-fi scenarios and the collective belief in fiction just might make it real.

Top Grossing Science Fiction Movies
1977 - 2011

Note: Adjusted for Ticket Price Inflation (not that you care).

Rank	Movie	Released	Inflation-Adjusted Gross Income
1	Star Wars Ep. IV: A New Hope	1977	$1,284,600,464
2	ET: The Extra-Terrestrial	1982	$1,060,155,772
3	Avatar	2009	$778,817,600
4	Star Wars Ep. V: The Empire Strikes Back	1980	$761,835,156
5	Star Wars Ep. VI: Return of the Jedi	1983	$733,586,163
6	Star Wars Ep. I: The Phantom Menace	1999	$669,453,553
7	Jurassic Park	1993	$668,021,841
8	Close Encounters of the Third Kind	1977	$587,327,355
9	Independence Day	1996	$546,452,224
10	Ghostbusters	1984	$518,616,036
11	Star Wars Ep. III: Revenge of the Sith	2005	$468,061,089
12	Back to the Future	1985	$443,824,169
13	Men in Black	1997	$429,990,822
14	Transformers: Revenge of the Fallen	2009	$423,021,687
15	Star Wars Ep. II: Attack of the Clones	2002	$410,363,011
16	The Lost World: Jurassic Park	1997	$393,768,629
17	Terminator 2: Judgment Day	1991	$378,305,349
18	The Matrix Reloaded	2003	$368,401,095
19	Transformers	2007	$365,912,289
20	2001: A Space Odyssey	1968	$341,498,475
21	Signs	2002	$309,556,860
22	Inception	2010	$292,576,223
23	I am Legend	2007	$291,623,655
24	Austin Powers in Goldmember	2002	$289,362,239
25	The War of the Worlds	2005	$288,369,109

Source: http://www.the-numbers.com/market/CreativeTypes/ScienceFiction.php

Of course there's more science fiction out there than on that list, but it gives a good idea of where to start from and in which direction to continue.

Star Wars: If you can't beat them, join them.

The maxim of the Romans when conquering all before them was 'divide and conquer' and Darth Vader and his evil empire seem to have the same stratagem surgically implanted in their heads. On the plus side, all empires need to trade. No trade, no empire. So if/when earth falls under the shadow of Darth Vader's Empire, we should be prepared to offer something, other than resistance. Naturally home grown Human Rights Campaigners, Anarchists, Lefties and the United States, will probably rebel and join Luke Skywalker and the resistance for lofty reasons, but let's be serious: The evils committed by Darth Vader need never concern you because you probably won't know of them, until of course it is way too late. Besides, earthlings don't have the technology to resist. Therefore, join the wining team, offer something of value. Open earth into a repair shop for Star Destroyers and give Jabba the Hut a second home in the Sahara Desert. For industrious countries and multinationals, open up a factory pumping out cloned storm troopers. Become a vital trading partner, and on the side, open a few inter-galactic brothels too. The Romans would be proud.

ET

An alien botanist is too slow to get back to his ship before it takes off and is chased by fighter jets. Life for an alien botanist is no walk in the grass. ET has to make a friend, build a contraption that he can call home with (get the ship back) and not die. He's probably not the first strange alien botanist on a strange alien planet to have to go through these trials. You'd expect it to be part of their training.

Apart from the heart-warming aspect of ET, the reality is quite plausible: Who should come from the stars but seekers of knowledge, and the most basic and readily available knowledge are of course plants. The biodiversity of the jungles would seem to offer a lot more avenues for discovery than the woods around outer suburbia (where ET was set, mainly to get suburbanites to see it) so if you or anyone else makes contact with alien botanists, make them feel at home. Send them to the far corners of the earth to discover things we haven't discovered yet.

Avatar

Somewhere in the future, us nasty earthlings are upsetting some lesser species on a world far, far away, all for commercial gain! This slight role reversal which forms the backdrop to Avatar is none other than a rehashing of chastising colonialism but in a space age when we actually made it far, far from our cosy Solar System. Well done earthlings.

The most thought provoking diplomatic point of view, is how are we really to present ourselves should we find intelligent life out there? Because we're hundreds, if not at least a thousand years, away from escaping our Solar System and making it somewhere that could possibly sustain life long enough to let billions of years take its course, we don't have to dwell too much on how we'd project our form of diplomacy on lesser aliens. In that respect, we don't have to grow up. We can be the invader, the conqueror, and the protector of other worlds.

Close Encounters of the Third Kind

Again, like ET, an easy to digest story is hugely successful: We want to believe, but we also want mysteries solved. In

Close Encounters of the Third Kind, the alien mother ship is coming, the world is facing a new reality, and the aliens are returning (among other things) missing planes into a desert, and then later on the pilots (who haven't aged a bit since their disappearance decades earlier) and are communicating through light and sound to government scientists.

And they're taking some of us away with them. Naturally we'd want the mother ship to stick around, besides, time cannot possibly be a problem to them, but that would ruin a good story and closing scenes. Close Encounters of the Third Kind is actually quite helpful in priming the masses for the complexities of any alien contact and therefore diplomacy: There is a hell of a lot of basic connecting to accomplish before we can do any meaningful talking.

War of the Worlds: The Classic and the most Potent

The nasty aliens bent on exterminating mankind are the most potent symbol of an alien invasion. There is no sentiment, no communication, not even blood lust. It appears they want to turn us into fertiliser for our planet. And yes, the funny thing is they may have deemed our feeble resistance laughable, but miscalculated the germs of our planet, which ultimately kills them off. What a plot spoiler! Imagine the Commander of the Invasion Force penning an email (or a tweet) to headquarters on Mars of wherever, the look on his face as he minces his words: "Dear Sirs, tried our best to take earth, met heavy resistance from evil microbe things that killed my best troops. Yours sincerely, Earth Invasion Commander. PS I resign. Time for an honourable suicide."

The reality is that any alien race that comes to exterminate us can and probably will. Therefore, there can be no diplomacy, it's a fight to the death. Now that we've accepted our destiny, it's worth noting that an invasion fleet is hurtling to us, 10 light years away, and closing in.

2001: A Space Odyssey

The classic and probably the most astute: Some super aliens have left markers in our Solar System for us to stumble over. The trouble is, we have to find them, and maybe they'll help us find our way. If there is a lesson about 2001: A Space Odyssey is that once a species is upright, walking and talking, and over fighting, space exploration will reward you, as long as you can get out there and do not trust your onboard HAL artificially intelligent and malevolent computer to do all your thinking for you. You can't really have a Space Age unless you have your Digital Age under control.

We're Part of a Space Opera

Space opera is a grand genre in written science fiction that combines the raciness of Flash Gordon and Shakespearian monologues. You'll find space opera in many sci-fi books, however books are fast becoming superseded by new technology like tablets. But, nothing will ever replace a good book, because nothing beats a good opera. The story of an opera is a spaghetti bowl full of characters; heroes, villains, heroines, alpha bitches, the unfortunate, the miserable, jokers and witches, kings and peasants. Space opera as a genre is an improvement on standard 'us' versus 'them' science fiction and certainly adds more social dimensions to the space time fabric. The question coming now is, what are we in the great space operas? Are we the hermit in the forgotten forest staring pleasantly at the sky? Are we the mute blind man stumbling around the country side the space opera heroes look upon with pity, and the space opera villains pass us by as not worth robbing? Our part in the space opera can only be found by getting out there.

Men in Black

Men in Black (MIB) is a top-secret agency that monitors alien activity on earth; earth is a "neutral zone" for alien refugees, and MIB answer to no government yet their funding comes from their interesting patents (much confiscated from aliens) Velcro, microwave ovens, and liposuction. The setting of the film (and the comic which came first) is the wet-dream of every alien believer: Not only are we not alone, but we're part of the action! Yes, we're part of the big screen action. If earth is part of the inter-galactic actions, the annoying cone of secrecy surrounding it should be broken down. Earth will be united when we see the diversity of species out there, looking down at us.

Aliens & Predator:
Shut Up and Play Along

With the nasty warrior creatures in Predator, it's always a fight to the death. According to the Predator movies, they like to hunt humans as a sport. They create game reserves and throw in some top hunters from all around the galaxy and hunt them down. So what happens if a motley crew of Predators turns up? Well, appease them with a theme-park. Turn an island into a little experiment for the Predators to run around in. Earth can dispose of its most potent criminals and fervent terrorists: if they want to go out in a ball of flames, let them try it against our new inter-galactic friends the Predators. Create live feeds of the action and get a cut from syndication deals that include Earth Rights, and Predator Species Rights – where ever and whoever they really are. Throw in some acid-blooded creature from Aliens too. Everyone needs a fighting chance.

Independence Day: Another Grizzly Fight to the Death

Pretty much the same premise of the War of the Worlds: Aliens come, they want to exterminate humans, and if not stopped will get their way. The plot spoiler for Independence Day is that some clever humans insert a clever computer virus into the evil alien mother ship! Of all the cheap plot devices to close an expensive story into a happy ending, this takes the cake.

In all fairness to an invading alien species, they should and would have all their bases covered. They would know their own weaknesses from past experience of wiping out species on other pretty little planets. They would have a pre-invasion checklist and stick to it rigorously.

The Earth Pre-Invasion Checklist

One. Confuse the Earthlings: Make them think an external hostile act comes from within, e.g. a geographic dispute not to be ignored (like unfair trade tariffs) that leads to World War Three or Four or Five or whenever we get there.

Two. Blind the Earthlings: Whatever technology they employ to see beyond their own belly buttons should be disabled and make it look like the work of some naturally occurring events, like a solar storm. Knock out all their satellites. Flip their magnetic poles around and see how their internet works.

Three. Divide the Earthlings: Again back to the first point, get them fighting themselves first. If they're united, they might actually enjoy mustering up the courage to repelling our Star Cruisers with their puny little nuclear weapons. Divide them by favouring some, pitting them against others, and then reversing the process.

Four. Liquidate the Earthlings: Concoct some nano-viral-creature that spreads via social butterfly air kisses around the world, lies dormant for a few months, and then causes a human to drown in its own mucus as it uncontrollably wets its pants, thereby inducing suffocation and shame to stop it from calling for help.

Five. Eradicate Human Existence: Wipe the face of the Earth clean with energy efficient solar-powered lasers: Destroy all buildings, infrastructure and human objects. Be careful not to injure any other animals, that would break the Universal Laws on Appropriate Genocide of Intelligent Yet Annoying Life forms (Chapter 2, Clause 5, section 3).

Six. Impregnate the cleansed earth with one's own experiment. Yes, this has been what's always been going on, but this time bring back the dinosaurs – they were more interesting to watch and more sporting to try and duel one-to-one.

X-Files

Mass market movies offer limited scope for Alien Diplomacy: It's all 90 minutes of fear and shoot outs. The artists (writers, actors and producers) have to earn a living, and serving up your worst fears of the future is like money for jam. Filling the intellectual void is of course a television series, allowing the artists to stretch a concept, and therefore their (employment) contract, much further, and really probe deep into space and our place out there.

The X-Files gave viewers odd alien creatures and a government conspiracy to hide them. Slogans like "The

Truth Is Out There" and "I Want to Believe" plus a renewed mistrust of secretive governments permeated into the mainstream culture. It is progress, so you may want to believe, but where the hell are these aliens?

Plot spoiler / reality check: We have to improve our chances of being worthwhile of contact, and then we can begin some diplomatic course that lifts us off this planet into a new enlightenment.

Star Trek

Star Trek is more television series than movies, so moving on the concept is simple: We get out there. We get so far out there with the Enterprise that we put on the cop uniform and with Captain Kirk keep peace in the universe. Boldly captivating science fiction, mixing frontier mentality with laser shoot outs, Star Trek keeps the baddies (the Klingons) in balance with the bio-diversity of the universe; all those odd looking aliens (not only do the writers get to work overtime, but the make-up artists too) making appearances. Star Trek is dreamy, because by the time we get out there, dealing with such complicated situations, artificial intelligence would be vastly more capable than Captain Kirk and his human-Vulcan sidekick Dr. Spock. Star Trek is drama, but hopefully one day we will be out there, "to explore strange new worlds, to seek out new life and new civilizations, to boldly go where no man has gone before."

Battlestar Gallactica

Battlestar Gallactica was first a one-series wonder in the 1980s and then re-done as several TV series with tie-in movies. The premise of Battlestar Gallactica is that humans on twelve colonies are wiped out by their own creation: Smart ass artificial intelligence Cylons. Some humans survive, and led by the Battlestar Gallactica, their motley crew of space craft escape into the deep vacuum of space to begin the search for a new place to call home: the fabled Earth. While eerily reminiscent of the Old Testament where feuding tribes of Jews are expelled and forced to wander the wastelands in search of the land of milk and honey, and escape the clutches of their Arab mates, Battlestar Gallactica plays on a primal notion that someone is looking for us, some lost tribe will one day be re-united with us. However, if some friends suddenly rock up in our orbit in a Battlestar, the first question we have to ask is, "Is anyone following you?"

Plot spoiler: When weary refugees eventually do find earth, they find it a nuked-out wasteland. However, they eventually find a nicer blue jewel, which is actually our earth, and mix with the hunter and gatherer natives, and form the basis of our race. So, we 'half' came from the stars.

How Can We Improve Our Chances?

Be the change you want to see in the world.

Mahatma Gandhi

In the wide and nearly unpredictable domain of Alien Diplomacy, the very question of 'How can we improve our chances?' sprouts a few more mind boggling but not totally impossible to answer questions.

Improve Our Chances of What?

Yes, good question. Thank your subconscious for dragging this up because although the width of the question falls into murky areas, the goal is pretty easy: We want to be valuable in the eyes of a space travelling species.

Without having to prove these space travelling species exist, you can sleep well at night assuming that as the universe is perhaps 10 billion years old, in that time, someone, somewhere, has mastered space travel, likes to travel, and likes to meet interesting people on their travels.

Valuable in What Way?

The first point to note is that we don't offer any value, yet. Earth may be valuable, but evidently we aren't worthy of an Alien Consulate.

If you can imagine our current lonely predicament where there is not, as far as we are informed, an inter-galactic space hub that allows earthlings the chance to visit other worlds that are home to other intelligent beings, then you assume we will always be cut off from the action, if it at all exists.

The first step to be totally useless in the eyes of extraterrestrials is to give up hope that there is intelligent life out there. As most of earth's inhabitants have plenty of other things to occupy their minds with, a reputable Earth Intergalactic Diplomatic School (sometimes referred to as Exopolitics) won't be forming for a while, or making that much of a profit to stay around. Also, sadly, there must be quite a few comfortable planets that mastered sustainability and peace and then decided not to pursue interplanetary journeys because the night sky looked empty and there was no identifiable target screaming at them to come and visit. Of these planets' histories before and after this moment, spanning the birth and death of this universe (if that's how it works), of those planets that never ventured to reach out, we will know nothing. Some far reaching inter-stellar species may discover artefacts from these slack civilisations, which will then be displayed in museums and the hallways (leading to the bathrooms) of private collectors around the universe, but it's a bit like the tree that falls in the forest: Does anyone hear it? If you stumble across it, laying across the path before you, you can only shrug your shoulders and step over it.

So, let's be valuable. Let's be worth discovering.

A Value to Ourselves Beyond the Basics

Humans are comfortable creatures. Just look at the suburban sprawls of the first world, and the shanty towns of the rest. If we don't have to be eating worms in the jungle, we'll gladly work 9 to 5 and chow down on fast food. Complacency is the demise of all great empires and it takes some imagination and money to reach beyond our own comfort zones.

President Kennedy did it with America's missions to the Moon. The Soviets and now the Russians keep up some sort of action, and countries with healthy economies do dip their toes into the cosmos. At the time of writing, there are nine guys who kicked up dust on an alien world. The twelve Apollo astronauts that landed on the moon were all born between the years 1923 and 1935 and all will most likely be dead by 2030. If you view those who kick dust on an alien planet as a group, then they are an endangered group, and therefore earth is an endangered planet: Less effort to get off the planet means we're more likely to die on it.

Yet getting off it costs. Estimates fly around that 1% of the US's gross domestic product was required to send 12 men to walk on the moon, and though that may seem a waste of money for researching an already known lifeless planet, the flow on effects helped kick-start innovation in the same way that wars force innovation, that in time filters down to our prosaic lives.

But how do you convince governments, tax payers, and voters, of the value of exploring the very great and very incomprehensible unknown when the value is hard to define. Satellites that serve earth are one step, a previous mission to the moon a good reminder, but what would pull the hearts of those that matter most – the voters and consumers.

Inter-galactic Credibility

Probably the biggest hurdle to adding space value to our planet, or inter-galactic credibility, is the goal itself. Who are we meant to impress and why? The 'Who' don't exist. There may be UFO sightings but there isn't a daft looking extraterrestrial tourist wearing a "I Love Earth" t-shirt, standing at the end of your street looking at an upside down map of your city, embarrassed to be lost but humbly waiting for a kind human to give them some directions and chit-chat. Most earthlings are more concerned about their daily lives than shelving out tax to projects that might gain earth some vague sense of inter-galactic credibility, but that is not to say inter-galactic credibility does not exist, now that billions of dollars is required to make it exist.

It already exists: It is the irrepressible desire to explore. The how, when, who and with what will come in due time, thanks to the same factors that built a series of empires that has resulted in our form of civilisation of today.

Show Me the Money

The commercialisation of space is hindered by gravity. Once we can escape earth's orbit we'll be off and running. The moon will be colonised. Space stations will be staffed. Some nutters will raise the money required to ship their dreamy minds off to Mars. But the biggest windfall will be the mining and commoditisation of materials found in asteroids and planets of the solar systems. This will create a new revolution, the type not seen since the discovery of the New World and the invention of the steam engine. The causes of wars on earth may be eradicated by the bounty from above; precious metals, abundant energy, space to explore rather than to fight over. We may be saved here on earth by the treasures in the sky yet to get there requires a certain kind of diplomacy from within.

It Starts with Us

The political unification of goals across national interests (the European Space Agency being somewhat of an example) and the commercial energy of private players (the

Google Lunar X PRIZE being another example) are a start but the vision needs to spread.

If all the diplomacy spent separating feuding tribes and evening scores (not just the bloody kind, but tit for tat trades disputes) was funnelled into developing a strategic and coherent plan to get our unique form of intelligence out into space to test ourselves and unlock immense value that would benefit us forever, and ever, then that's a proper start.

Until there is consensus and diplomacy within, we won't be attractive to an alien species. Getting over ourselves is the hardest task. And then we're faced, at some point in the future, with a crisis.

When we do come across an alien species, next year, next century or in a thousand years, what the hell are we going to talk to them about?

What We Need to Ask Them

Who are we? We find that we live on an insignificant planet of a humdrum star lost in a galaxy tucked away in some forgotten corner of a universe in which there are far more galaxies than people.

Carl Sagan

When we really meet with them, chances are that our most distinguished and articulate people capable of the job will not be there. It could be, for better or for worse, someone like you. Whoever is lucky or scared enough to be in the right time at the right place, they'll need a cool head in order to enable clear thinking communication. We need to 'filter' our spacezoid guests in order to understand them, and ultimately us.

Interpret Their Intentions

We on earth are like the poor family on the street that is the last to have everything: The last to embrace new cool technology, fashion, art and helpful kitchen appliances, because we're just lagging behind, like the dumbest kid in the classroom, who will never pick up the advanced stuff (like travelling through worm holes – what civilisation hasn't mastered that after 5,000,000 years of seasoned space travel?). Our exploits are practically nil compared to the interstellar civilisation that manages to get here, and upon meeting them here, we have to ask ourselves what are their intentions? This is not so easy, but the answer does surface once you have some evidence about the visitor.

Communication (Breakdown)

Expect initial communication to be tiresome. First of all, if they haven't studied up any of the world's major languages, we're at a loss. If we start on an even playing field, we'll have to cooperate to develop the tools (probably a piece of software) to enable us to connect. And with any tool, there are bugs, leading to communication problems. In any case, the forestalment of communication creates time in which a bond can be built, so hopefully after we've worked out what they're on about, they don't feel like eating us anyway.

Alien Diplomacy Checklist(s)

What we need to ask them is our filtering method to gauge exactly what we mean to them.

Where are you from and how far have you travelled?

A sense of location and distance may not be of any consequence because we may have no idea of where their starting point is, other than as a dot of light amid a shimmering sea of stars in some murky corner of the galaxy our humble Hubble Telescope hasn't got around to viewing because its funding was allocated to some charity pit in Africa. In any case, they need to be from somewhere and we'll need to record that. If they answer, "Oh, we're from Mars" then we must respond, "Oh, yes we knew that... Um what we meant was where on Mars. North or south of the equator? How is the weather there this time of year?"

Of the duration of you journey here and back to your home, how much is that of a proportion to your expected life time?

Get this question sorted out straight away. The old sea faring explorers and traders sailing around the world could expect to be away for three years, and in those days life expectancy was a lot lower too, not to mention the success rate of such voyages. Death on the voyage might be 50%, and the voyage might take 10% of your life, or even 20% of your working life. That's bravery.

In our merry lives, to take a jumbo jet to the other side of the world (2 days), and then travel by car to a remote destination (3 days) and then hike to an extremely remote destination (2 days) and stay there for a week, and then go home, the same way would equal three weeks. If you can expect to live 82.5 years, then a three week exploration, though a highlight of your life, can never really compare to a three year voyage (into the real unknown) that your forefathers may have signed up to, or been press-ganged into.

If we identify that a visiting party of Aliens have invested their life in a visit to us, our respect and gratitude to them must be withheld until we clarify: But are you just robots?

Are you just Robots?

"Good question!" will probably be the response, "But don't insult us!"

Although to us a Yes (do you run on batteries) / No (must have been a long trip, here have a beer) answer would suffice, the reality may be something completely different. An advanced species would clone or manufacture their best for a Mission to Earth. However, a Robot Alien might just as easily judge us as Robot Humans, judging by our predominantly template habits. They can easily argue that there are simply not that many truly creative and competent people on our earth to justify that we are totally beyond robotic behaviour.

How many of you exist, and what proportion of you travel this far?

Earth has a population of 7 billion. Twelve of them have kicked dust on the Moon. Maybe another 500 have been in space, either as astronauts or space tourists. Space travel of any kind is rare. For an Alien Species, they may live in space, they may colonise space, and would therefore have a higher number of space faring citizens (if they are all citizens – some could very well be slaves). Perhaps they are like us, space travel is rare, therefore the meeting is very unique. However, if all of them embark on space travel, perhaps the visitor has simply lost his way, stumbled upon earth, and hasn't worked out what to do. Perhaps it is a she, on the run from the police. Half our luck.

How do you travel? Can I look under the hood?

Interstellar notions of benevolence may crumble at this question.

"Sorry earthlings, we can't show you what motors our cigar shaped space ship. Besides, you wouldn't understand it."

"Understand it or not, we want one."

And from here on it gets tricky. Are they here to offer us a temporary or a permanent ride off our planet to explore the cosmos, or are they visiting a poor neighbourhood in a Rolls-Royce because they can. A transfer of advanced technology could wreak damage to humanity, so any intelligent species has to think cautiously about letting us play with their ray guns.

Who else is out there?

An obvious question but the nature of how we ask it can tell way too much about ourselves. We want to know, but we don't want them to know that we're the last to know of all that's out there. It's a bit like looking around the poker table to see who the sucker is, and if you can't work out who it is, then it's you. We'll be taking Game Theory to the intergalactic level. Will we be ashamed of our innocence or act the social butterfly, "So, tell me Alien Visitor, what do you really think of the other interstellar civilisations?"

"Which one are you referring to, earthling?"

"Um, my neighbours?"

"We are your neighbours."

"Oh. So... Seen any new black holes recently? Fascinating, are they not?"

Can you lend me some money, or, do you want a loan?

There's no better way to shore up a relationship than to make it contractual, and as money has greased so many of the wheels that have carried our civilisation this far, keep the wagon going! By elevating Earth-to-Alien communication to a commercial relationship we are, in their minds, not just potentially the last planet to lend money to in the known universe, but expressing an interest in the wider universe. We must offer commerce on a wider scale, other than that of some basic battering we've seen between 18th Century explorers and native populations of untamed wildernesses. Scale-up our deals, even to our detriment – it can only speed up the ultimate consequence. Look at the financial calamity in the early 21st century: The high profile borrowers gained more prestige and power.

Perhaps the most grandiose position is to offer to lend money to a visitor from space. Detractors of cash-for-alien-contacts may cry and wail and beat their little fists on the girly chests, "Really, do you think money will be important to a species 1 billion years old?" but who cares? It's important to us, so let's share it. Share it all around the universe, print as much of it as possible – it's what our governments do anyway.

Scaring us into Action

The mental walls that keep us in, keeps 'them' out, so before we can see them we have to see ourselves in a new light. History has shown that an outside fear can act as a catalyst to unite and accomplish great things, so perhaps the best thing that can happen to earth is bad diplomacy with aliens.

It is plausible that there is an alien drone, possibly dormant (sleeping on the job if it is a government drone) and slowly waking up to our technological advances. It's also possible an alien species has sent a mother ship to our solar system, parked it out of sight (like on the other side of the sun) and sends what we call UFOs down to check on our progress. How do we respond? With scrambled fighter jets, frothing internet forums, denial, cover ups, creative meanderings, some very non-creative speculation, and then the issue dies away as something closer to home drains our attention, like a celebrity divorce or a clash of barbarians in the Middle East.

We should be interested, but most of us are not. We should be rational, but some of us need the entertainment. We will face up to an alien species looking down on us, and perhaps our inability to prepare ourselves will be the shock required to wake us up. Our lack of diplomacy and tact may trigger us into a new awareness. The unintended consequence of an alien visitation will be a change in ourselves – the ultimate checking (as in a slap on the face) of our inter-galactic innocence.

Conspiracy, Cover-Up, and Caution

"I think about how quickly our differences worldwide would
vanish if we were facing an alien threat from outside
this world. And I ask you,
does not this threat already exist?"

President Ronald Reagan

Conspiracy by the Camp Fire

The expressions on the fire-lit face of the story-teller
applies the glowing paint to the shapes of the ghosts he has
successfully seeded in our imagination through well practiced
narratives – we are not suckers, we just want to believe. We
want a higher purpose, a connection to an 'other world'.
Before the modern age there were an abundance of creatures
that lurked in our collective imaginations: Goblins, Trolls,
Elves, Sea Monsters. Even porky tax collectors had personas,
now they're just faceless public servants. Of all the slithering
creatures that have roamed earth, Dragons were and are
perhaps the most well documented because statues and
stories are testament to their existence; after being inoculated
by so much dragon paraphernalia, how can they not exist?
Well, we grow older, and we see that there still aren't any
dragons soaring above our heads, hosing flames in their
wake, stealing the prettiest of virgins.

What we do have are UFOs, less mythical and more mechanical, which leads to the questions of who are they, what are they doing here, and with whom. A trickle of 'sightings' and concepts of life from out there form a torrent of wondering; so many wild imaginations, so many possibilities, not only do we want to believe, we have to believe. Among the congestion of conspiracy theories, what is the most believable? Surely they can't all be true, and surely if one is partially correct, but which one?

Thanks to the internet's zero cost to 'publish and push' information, and the ease at which photographs and video can be doctored by the digital 'believing' generation with too much time on their hands (shouldn't they be outside playing sport, chasing girls, or practising throwing stones at invading aliens?), there is an oversupply of UFO material, and this avalanche of material is linked by one narrative: They're out there. That's it. We believe. Our desire to believe ever more than before drives the creators of hoax UFO video clips to sharpen their skills even more.

On the other hand, pre-digital age, most early UFO sightings come about during World War Two and onwards. Up until the 1960s, it was normal to assume, thanks to the importance of religion governing peoples' lives, that according to the scriptures, God created us and we are alone. He spent six days creating us, and now it's the seventh day and He relaxes, watches all the biblical movies we've churned out in His honour, and scrutinizes our prayers. Western society, at least, until the 1960s, was God fearing. To a government in this period facing the hard reality that we are not alone, and that superior aliens can prove that anytime they wish by buzzing an airport or jamming a nuclear missile silo, the concept of 'aliens out there coming here' unleashed on the general public could have quite unforeseen outcomes.

Hence the logic in the possible government conspiracy to hide 'a' truth.

When it comes to governments and the truth, we accept that their truth is flawed every time their new budget is released. We are ready to swallow macro-economic fallacies because we have little time to don our accounting hat and scrutinise our government's account balances.

Yet when it comes to governments and UFOs, the truth is somewhat deeper and abstract. We don't have the time, nor the intelligence, to don our scientist, theologian, politician, and behavioural physiologist hats to map out the impact of telling all the peoples of the worlds that God doesn't exist like you think he/she/it does because he/she/it does/doesn't exist for these things over here: These funny looking green men calling the shots from their upside-down spinning hub-cups.

So, if UFOs were aliens and they did land or crash and make contact and take coffee and share a joke with Presidents, clandestine shadow governments and anyone else lucky enough to be in on the deal, deny it, because to admit it, and this means retracting so much false information, would also de-stabilise the trust and pact we have with our governments; elected politicians, career public servants, and the military. And they don't want that. Deep down you don't want that either. You don't want widespread anarchy to break out because a full-de-classification reveals the full extent of betrayal, and the irate people take up pitch-forks and shotguns and start a revolution. It's upsetting to our dreary routines but would make great 24-7 news coverage, if only it lasted just 24 hours.

But, if you can imagine a government, or several governments, concealing the truth from the public, without stretching the imagination too far, what could they really be covering up?

Covering Up What?

There is a tonne of 'evidence' online that is not worth mentioning, is somewhat entertaining, but if congested too frequently will interfere with your ability to converse normally with people at work and at parties without saying things like, "Did you know that the 2012 apocalypse predicted by the Mayans may actually be a cover by the reptilians – a breed of aliens in power for thousands of years that shape shift and are actually running our counties and economies (Obama, Putin, maybe Ghandi – All reptilians) – to keep us from really understanding that it was ancient astronauts that seeded mankind and may make a comeback to avert the catastrophe of the new world order?"

"But, 2012 was last year."

"Oh."

Yes, Oh. Oh what are they on about.

At the other end of the believable scale, that is heading towards people who know better than to spin tales, and who may have been fortunate to live their boyhood dreams and fly fast machines, push the envelope and escape earth, are astronauts.

Buzz Aldrin, the second man to walk on the moon, has even publicly stated that something was following Apollo 11 on its way to the moon. Gordon Cooper, one of the seven original astronauts from Project Mercury, the first manned space effort by the United States, after seeing UFOs twice as a pilot, even went as far as writing a letter to the United Nations advising that some kind of office be set up to collate information about UFOs. The sixth man to walk on the moon, Edgar Mitchell, also believes that aliens craft have crashed on earth, knowledge of such events are suppressed, and a government cover-up is in place. The cover-up, in place by the U.S. Government, all in the name of security, was to hide the existence of UFOs while at the same time extract technology from alien space craft.

If the conspiracy is true, and there is a cover-up, what we have are top level military or a sub-section of the military controlling contact with aliens. You may shudder that nothing is as it seems, but relax. If all this is true, there's one word to describe the conspiracy: Sleazy. Or two words: Sleazy Bitches.

Now the questions comes to mind: What on earth are aliens doing talking to just the military? It is like some extra-marital affair where a seductive alien and a fatty general are lying in bed...

The alien whispers in the general's ear, "So when are you going to tell her (the public)?"

The general stubs out a post-coital cigar, exhales, and sighs to the sky, "Damn it, she (they) wouldn't understand, she's too fragile. It would ruin everything."

The alien sighs, "I can't go on like this... We must tell her... I fell so, well..."

"What, darling?"

"I don't like being kept in the dark..."

"But darling..." the general wails, "Why ruin what we have, together, forever?"

Don't these aliens have a sense of humour, or guilt? Or, there could be more than one type of alien our very secretive governments are mindful of: Aliens, inter-planetary, inter-stellar, inter-galactic, or inter-dimensional visit us, may even look like us, and could easily have wiped us out. So if there are several types of aliens, does one of them have the sense of humour that frees them to engage in dialogues with people other than secretive and non-accountable government and military types?

Hold Your Horses

Catch your breath. There is a conspiracy. There is a cover up. And extra terrestrials can't be bothered to get in contract with anyone but the military, or some secret shadow government. Sometimes it's better to disbelieve the un-provable and have a nice drink. Does this mean that the rest of us are not credible, not cool enough, or better off kept in the dark to wander with our feeble imaginations?

Or, does it mean aliens have a keen and watchful eye on the generals and the powers that be, because somewhere, something grave could have happened: Nuclear wipe out.

If there is a 'Secretive Government Cover Up' they're probably hiding more than just the detailed knowledge of the existence of aliens, they may also have more formidable things to hide, like their ineptitude to dismantle the apparatus that could smother earth in a radioactive cloud and the fact that aliens want to make sure that never happens, and the other fact that if earth is watched by one group of aliens, there should be others out there. At some point, earth becomes a commodity worth appropriating and the military can't do a single thing to protect earth, except deny that there is the remotest of threats.

Now that we live in a somewhat enlightened age, vibrant with communication of both the mundane and amazing, we'll believe anything. If there is a conspiracy, a cover-up, and caution to spill the beans on the public, what part of it had actual aliens to play in this?

They seem to have the right to fly alongside commercial passengers jets, zoom over remote areas and scare earthling peasants, and hover around airports. What are they after, duty-free offers? If they're so 'Top Secret' yet according to the moderate believers, 'out there and not too far away at all', then the secret is partially out and someone looks like a fool:

Not the public, not the military (who are just doing their job etc) but visiting aliens.

Why they are so non-communicative to the general earth populace is probably due to their in-ability to relate with us. After all, we have very little idea of how to relate to them – the problem is mirrored. Hence a stalemate. A bit like at a bus stop where the bus is late, no one knows anyone, tedious boredom sets in – how to get the conversation going?

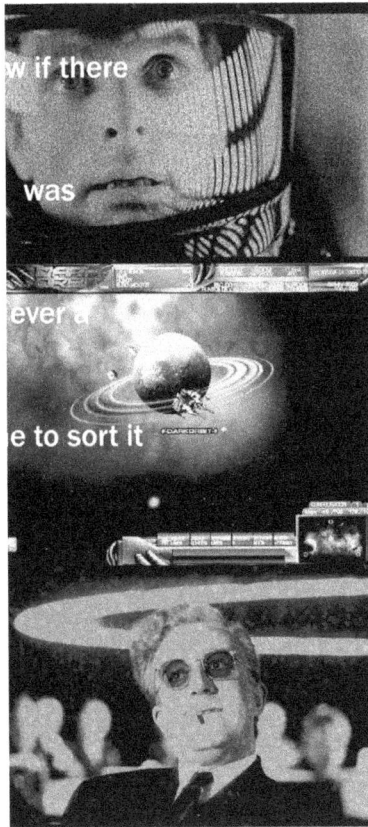

The Time is Now

Why we are not involved in an active and very public diplomacy with aliens could be because they are or were in a clandestine relationship with a 'secret government', or because they're anti-social, shy, maybe even too cool. The sad truth may be so simple: They don't know what to say. They may have seen civilisations come and go and when it comes to earth, they're above our skies, looking down, a bit puzzled, a bit amused, laying bets, computing risk analysis, wondering if we'll make it out of earth alive, not in the next ten or a hundred years, but in ten thousand or a hundred thousand years.

To aliens, the use of time is the ultimate diplomacy. If, in an infinite universe, with infinite possibilities, time is not so infinite (if there was a big bang, when is the big crunch?), then time is the crucial element. We are victims of time. It runs, and runs out. Aliens have had more time to survive themselves (their own evolution, planet, and scuffles), explore space, and ruminate on it all, while we, up until a few thousand years ago, were running around half naked setting each other's matted hair on fire. Yes it's obvious we're only just beginning a serious giant leap, but it is still up to us when we do it, not why.

When vs. Why

Arguing for space exploration (or even more space education) as a conclusion is like preaching to the converted, yet sometimes the converted need a shepherd, a guiding light, a manifesto, a vision, or plainly, a new tact.

The early 21st century has been marked by two oddities.

A war on terrorism. The war on terrorists has had such an insignificant body count it seems like a sideshow compared to conflicts of before. The West may or may not succeed in bringing democracy to backward lands, but the cost to try it is phenomenal. Why not spend some of that money on rocketing democracy to Mars? Set up a colony on an alien world and then see what the religious fanatics think about the West's prowess.

Climate change. The earth is no stranger to climate change. Our ancestors made it through one Ice Age and our descendants will make it through another. Man made climate change is a bizarre sideshow: There is a lot of political and moralist aggression surrounding a natural occurrence. Yet how much of global warming or even global cooling is caused by human activities is anyone's guess. Is it 1%, 5%, 50%, 100%? The rhetoric and energy to police hot air is commendable because we should enforce zero pollution and implement renewable electricity, but demonising nuclear power is not the answer. Next generation nuclear technology may get us out of the Sun's orbit, and the technology designed to outpace nuclear technology will get us to the stars, but demonising one form of energy creation is not a long term solution.

The 'why' argument has been buried by local annoyances (terrorism, climate change). There is no reason why we should even argue why we should explore space. However, some people shouldn't even be consulted; some are better left to toiling the soil / fattening themselves before a soap opera. The argument should not even be presented to intelligent people that have been sidetracked by fashionable causes – a determined mind is hard to sway. For the believers in Space

Exploration and the inevitable and real diplomacy with aliens, there is no need for a why, it's just a matter of when.

Accelerating the When: Space Commercialisation

Before the rise of any new industry there was a momentum.

To establish proper contact with an alien race requires a credible move by humanity to prove its desire to explore space.

To explore space requires a credible injection of genuine interest (sorry, watching blockbuster science fiction movies is not genuine, but reading a sci-fi book is getting there) and therefore investment into a commercially viable space industry.

True Space Commercialisation is not the use of satellites to beam back and forth information across the globe, that would be akin to saying merchant ships sailing around the British Aisle constituted the British Empire. Space Commercialisation is going into space, finding something of use, and extracting money from earthlings in exchange for it. The product may be rare minerals, the service may be a trip to the moon. In any case, all this will happen, but for it to happen in your lifetime requires an active investment of interest and money.

Make the Aliens Proud

Space commercialisation is easy to say, harder to implement. Whole sub-industries have to be created and without much of a cause that isn't that inseparable from a desire; a desire easy to shoot to pieces by anyone convinced of other needier things. For example, the creation of an 'alien world' colony complete with hotel requires tonnes of money. If your neighbouring country was experiencing famine (because they haven't mastered some basics tenets of civilisation (excluding the impact of things way out of their control)) do you cancel the Moon Base to feed a few million? Arguments will be raised like "The moon won't disappear, get to it later!" easily counteracted by, "There will always be another famine, trust me."

There is no end to the stand off – however, to embark on any venture requires sacrifice. World War Two, a monstrosity and a tragedy, was also a morally just cause to improve so much technology that the world was pulled up and away and set on a new path. Yet that is a path that we can always alleviate ourselves from – the Middle Ages followed the decline of the Roman Empire: What's a thousand years of relatively little technological advancement when we've been tooling axe heads for a few hundred thousand years?

The point is simple: We are going to explore space, and we'll have to pay for the privilege. And if we have to pay for the privilege, someone out there has been through all the agony and ecstasy long before us. When we bite the bullet and make the leap, then the Aliens will be proud.

The Search for Life

Life outside of earth is not just crawly things threatening your planet's independence with a ray gun at the end of each tentacle. The existence of life, outside of earth, is a source of inspiration that transcends so much of our mundane daily rituals that each new finding in the soil of Mars is nearly, not always, front page news.

Even when one form of alien life is found in the red soil, or in condensed gas plumes of Jupiter, it will only whet the appetite for more. What we eventually discover in each of the planets and their moons, and in the asteroid belts, of the solar system, will be eclipsed by what we can discover in neighbouring star systems. Human inquisitiveness will conquer space.

World War Three, or Four... Ten?

Contrary to the blesses and prayers of many, there is always going to be a time for a war or two, maybe next year, and certainly for the next several thousand years. Earth still has 'issues' to resolve, and the duration and the body counts in the future wars may differ, but the technological improvements should hopefully and consistently march on. Space is the next obvious battle ground. There will be an arms race in space that will transform space like how aerial warfare revolutionised civilian air travel. Space combat will require the invention of some truly space age kit, and one day, just maybe, our great-great-grandchildren can buy it off the shelf.

Superiority in an earth-bred space war will rely on having space craft with greater range, velocity (and braking), manoeuvrability and yes, highly accurate weapons. The future is up to robotic drones or Top Gun astronauts, or both, making an appearance, yet they don't have to blow each other apart into dangerously earth-orbiting space debris to do any good for the world. Their invention and use, like nuclear arsenals, may keep the peace.

Precious elements out there...

The technology in your pocket is not just data, it's resources. At some point the precious metals used in all the complicated pieces of junk (it's all junk in the end, or an artefact to someone else) need to be sourced from somewhere else other than open-cut mines carved into rainforests. Environmental conservation may inadvertently force us to look way up and away rather than down. Besides, why tear up earth's bio-diversity when you can dig up a lifeless asteroid or sweep the dust off a crater and pick up the sparkling goodies? And if you've got the means to extract minerals from Io, why not reach out to a distant star? Return on investment will be a key fundamental, but once the cost to explore diminishes, so too the time to cover great distances, and a shift in profit goals to something like fifty years rather than a quarter year is acceptable, those precious minerals will be a lot more affordable.

Space Tourists to the Rescue...

Given a price entry point that suits your budget, who wouldn't want to go into space, even if it's low orbit? The future will get us way out there, further and further. The good news for today is that there is demand, there are businesses making progress, and there will be new developments. But let's put the brakes on for a second. Think of a space hotel. Think of a space toilet. Think of sex in space. Think of getting drunk in space. We may master some of space, but to really have some space credibility (in the eyes of aliens) we have to master some of the basics first. Perhaps when we do meet with aliens and invite them on a TV chat show, the first inappropriate yet obviously appropriate question will be, "So tell me, Argar the 565435256th from Planet Boobtube, how do you defecate when you're travelling at half the speed of light for 42 years?"

They've Left a Little Surprise for Us...

Given time, we will explore space by our own steam.

Our own impetus is enough, but effort is rewarded in mysterious ways too. Like a child exploring a garden we will find things that attract our interest yet can only really recognise what we've found when we're older. We may seek a beacon from aliens and then realise it was always there. We may search in vain, endure all the poetic pain, and find nothing, that in total, comes to mean more than everything.

We may even discover out there, something about them, that they've long forgotten.

All we have to do is get out there, make contact, make the Aliens proud of us, and then comes the real diplomacy: Can we hitch a ride, further out into the universe?

The End

Simon Drake
Brisbane
March 2012